THE FANTASIAS FOR VIHUELA

RECENT RESEARCHES IN THE MUSIC OF THE RENAISSANCE

James Haar and Howard Mayer Brown, general editors

A-R Editions, Inc., publishes six quarterly series—

Recent Researches in the Music of the Middle Ages and Early Renaissance,
Margaret Bent, general editor;

Recent Researches in the Music of the Renaissance,
James Haar and Howard Mayer Brown, general editors;

Recent Researches in the Music of the Baroque Era,
Robert L. Marshall, general editor;

Recent Researches in the Music of the Classical Era,
Eugene K. Wolf, general editor;

Recent Researches in the Music of the Nineteenth and Early Twentieth Centuries,
Rufus Hallmark, general editor;

Recent Researches in American Music,
H. Wiley Hitchcock, general editor—

which make public music that is being brought to light
in the course of current musicological research.

Each volume in the *Recent Researches* is devoted
to works by a single composer or to a single genre of composition,
chosen because of its potential interest to scholars and performers,
and prepared for publication according to the standards that govern
the making of all reliable historical editions.

Subscribers to this series, as well as patrons of subscribing institutions,
are invited to apply for information about the "Copyright-Sharing Policy"
of A-R Editions, Inc., under which the contents of this volume
may be reproduced free of charge for study or performance.

Correspondence should be addressed:

A-R EDITIONS, INC.
315 West Gorham Street
Madison, Wisconsin 53703

RECENT RESEARCHES IN THE MUSIC OF THE RENAISSANCE • VOLUME LIV

Esteban Daza

THE FANTASIAS FOR VIHUELA

Edited by John Griffiths

A-R EDITIONS, INC. • MADISON

Copyright © 1982, A-R Editions, Inc.

ISSN 0486-123X

ISBN 0-89579-166-8

Library of Congress Cataloging in Publication Data:

Daza, Esteban, 16th cent.
   [Parnasso. Libro primero]
   The fantasias for vihuela.

   (Recent researches in the music of the
Renaissance , ISSN 0486-123X ; v. 54)
   Edited principally from the copy of the composer's
El parnasso (1576) in the Bayerische Staatsbibliothek,
Munich.
   Tablature and 2-stave transcription.
   1. Vihuela music.   I. Griffiths, John, 1952-
II. Series.
M2.R2384   vol. 54   [M142.V53]   82-13944
ISBN 0-89579-166-8

Contents

Preface		
	The Composer	vii
	The Source	vii
	The Music	xi
	Editorial Methods	xiv
	Performance Notes	xiv
	Critical Notes	xv
	Acknowledgments	xvii
	Notes	xvii
Plate I		xix
Plate II		xx

The Fantasias for Vihuela
Two-stave Transcription

[1.]	Fantasia por el primer tono	1
[2.]	Fantasia por el segundo tono	3
[3.]	Fantasia por el tercero tono	5
[4.]	Fantasia por el quarto tono	7
[5.]	Fantasia por el quinto tono	9
[6.]	Fantasia por el sexto tono	11
[7.]	Fantasia por el septimo tono	13
[8.]	Fantasia por el octauo tono	14
[9.]	Fantasia a tres, por el primer tono	16
[10.]	Fantasia a tres, por el quinto tono	18
[11.]	Fantasia a tres, por el septimo tono	20
[12.]	Fantasia a tres, por el octauo tono	22
[13.]	Fantasia por el primer tono	24
[14.]	Fanta[sia] por el pri[mer] tono, por gesolreut	26
[15.]	Fa[n]ta[sia] por el segu[ndo] tono, por gesolreut	28
[16.]	Fanta[sia] por [el] quarto tono, por alamire	30
[17.]	Fantasia por el sexto tono	32
[18.]	Fantasia por el primer tono	34
[19.]	Fantasia [de passos largos] por el primer tono	36
[20.]	Fantasia [de passos largos] por el mismo [= primer] tono	38
[21.]	Fantasia [de passos largos] por el quinto tono	40
[22.]	Fantasia [de passos largos] por el octauo tono	42

The Fantasias for Vihuela
Tablature

[1.]	Fantasia por el primer tono	47
[2.]	Fantasia por el segundo tono	48
[3.]	Fantasia por el tercero tono	50
[4.]	Fantasia por el quarto tono	51
[5.]	Fantasia por el quinto tono	53
[6.]	Fantasia por el sexto tono	55
[7.]	Fantasia por el septimo tono	56

[8.]	Fantasia por el octauo tono	57
[9.]	Fantasia a tres, por el primer tono	58
[10.]	Fantasia a tres, por el quinto tono	60
[11.]	Fantasia a tres, por el septimo tono	61
[12.]	Fantasia a tres, por el octauo tono	63
[13.]	Fantasia por el primer tono	65
[14.]	Fanta[sia] por el pri[mer] tono, por gesolreut	66
[15.]	Fa[n]ta[sia] por el segu[ndo] tono, por gesolreut	68
[16.]	Fanta[sia] por [el] quarto tono, por alamire	69
[17.]	Fantasia por el sexto tono	71
[18.]	Fantasia por el primer tono	72
[19.]	Fantasia [de passos largos] por el primer tono	74
[20.]	Fantasia [de passos largos] por el mismo [= primer] tono	76
[21.]	Fantasia [de passos largos] por el quinto tono	78
[22.]	Fantasia [de passos largos] por el octauo tono	80

Preface

The twenty-two fantasias in this edition make up the *libro primero* (i.e., the first section) of the vihuela book *El Parnasso* (Valladolid, 1576) by the Spanish composer and vihuelist Esteban Daza. These works are Daza's only extant original compositions.

The Composer

Esteban Daza is known to us only through his *El Parnasso*. No biographical details about him have emerged from any other source. The composer is described on the title page of his book as a *vecino* of Valladolid, a citizen, and thus a taxpayer, of that town. Genealogical sources confirm the surname Daza to be of noble lineage,[1] but it has not been possible to substantiate whether Esteban himself was a nobleman. No dates of his life are known. The date of publication for his *El Parnasso*, leads one to believe that Daza was probably born sometime between 1520 and 1555, and he died sometime between 1576, the year of publication of *El Parnasso*, and 1630. Although it is known that several other vihuelists held court positions, there are no records suggesting that Daza was ever employed as a court musician. This strengthens the possibility that he lived from independent means, and thus that he was a member of a wealthy or noble family. Even though Daza addressed himself to Hernando de Hábalos de Sotomayor as "your servant" in the dedication of *El Parnasso* (see translation below), the rhetorical nature of the statement makes it impossible to regard it as a clarification of Daza's position of employment or professional status. The compositions in *El Parnasso* reveal Daza as an inspired yet conservative musical personality. This music was composed by a man who was eloquent and fluent in his music expression, who was competent and thorough as a composer, and who was probably an advanced instrumental technician. Nobleman or not, the genius of Daza's work befits a professional musician of the highest caliber; he was certainly not a mere musical dilettante.

The Source

El Parnasso is an anthology of music for the vihuela and the last book of tablature known to have been printed for that instrument. Daza's collection appeared twenty-two years after its immediate predecessor, Miguel de Fuenllana's *Orphénica Lyra* (1554), and forty years after the earliest vihuela book, Luis Milán's *El Maestro* of 1536.[2] *El Parnasso* was the only vihuela book published during the reign of Philip II. Five copies of *El Parnasso* (all from the same printing) are known to be extant. Copies are held by the Bayerische Staatsbibliothek, Munich; the Biblioteca Publica Municipal, Porto; the Biblioteca Nacional, Lisbon (a defective copy); and the Biblioteca Nacional, Madrid (two copies, one defective).[3]

El Parnasso comprises 120 folios measuring approximately 205 x 145 mm. There are 114 folios of music, each page carrying three hexagram (six-line) staves of so-called Italian lute tablature (see Plate II). The book is divided into three sections called *libros*, each of which is devoted to works of a particular genre. Although a different number of works is contained in each one, the three *libros* are of approximately equal length. The total number of works in *El Parnasso* is sixty-two. The *libro primero* contains the twenty-two fantasias edited here. The *libro segundo* consists of intabulations by Daza of thirteen motets by Simon Boyleau, Crecquillon, Maillard, Richafort, Pedro and Francisco Guerrero, and Juan Basurto. Twenty-five Spanish secular pieces and two French chansons make up the *libro tercero*.[4] With the exception of the last two intabulations for solo vihuela in the *libro segundo*, all the works in the second and third *libros* are intended to be performed as accompanied solo songs, even though they are notated only in tablature. The voice to be sung in each of these works has the relevant tablature ciphers marked with *puntillos*, (i.e., apostrophes).

The source print begins with four unnumbered folios that precede the music and contain the title page, license, dedication, epigram, explanation of the tablature, and list of errata.[5] The epigram is in Latin, but all the remaining prefatory material is in Spanish. Two unnumbered folios follow the tablature and contain the table of contents and colophon. The explanation of tablature in *El Parnasso* is a variant of that given by Narváez in *Los seys libros del Delphín* (1538), and it reflects the fact that both books were made by the same printer. Most of Narváez's explanation is quoted verbatim by Daza, although Daza omits Narváez's discussion of syncopation, tempo, proportional signatures, and modes.⁶ The introductory folios of *El Parnasso*, omitting the list of errata and table of contents, are translated below:

Fol. I: Title Page [reproduced as Plate I]

Book of music in tablature for Vihuela, called *El Parnasso*, in which one will find all kinds of music, such as motets, sonnets, *villanescas* in the Castilian tongue and other things such as Fantasias by the author, made by Esteban Daça, citizen of the most notable town of Valladolid, dedicated to the most illustrious gentleman, the learned [*licenciado*] Hernando de Hábalos de Sotomayor, of the Supreme Council of His Majesty, etc. Printed by Diego Fernández de Córdoba, printer to His Majesty, in the year 1576. Priced at [added by hand in the Munich exemplar] 136 *maravedís*.

Fol. I[v]: Printing License

The King:

Whereas a request has been made on behalf of you, Esteban Daza, a citizen of the City of Valladolid, informing us that you had made a book of music for the vihuela which was very useful and beneficial; and considering the labors which you have put into it, besought us to command a license to be issued for its printing, and privilege of copyright for twenty years, or as should seem good to us. Which matter having been seen by our council, inasmuch as the said book has been subjected to due process as determined by our recently established ordinance on these matters, it was agreed that we should command our permit to that effect be issued, to which I have assented; we therefore grant our license and authority so that you, or any person empowered by you, and no other person whatever, may cause to be printed and sold the aforementioned book in these our Realms for time and space of ten full years immediately following, to run and be counted from the date of this permit, under penalty that whomever, not being by you so empowered, should print it, or sell it, or cause it to be printed and sold, suffer confiscation of the entire impression, together with the plates and equipment used therein, and furthermore incur as fine, fifty thousand *maravedís* for each and every offense, half of which is to be for our treasury and revenue and the other half for you, the said Esteban Daza; and on all occasions on which the said book is to be printed for the space of the said ten years, that it be laid before our council together with the original which was seen by them, and with every page initialed, and at the end of the whole, signed by Alonso de Vallejo, scrivener to the treasury, and resident upon our council, in order that it may be seen whether the said impression conforms to the original, and see if a license may be issued to you for its printing and for the fixing of the price at which each volume ought to be sold, under pain of incurring the penalties set forth in the said ordinance and laws of our Realms. And we command those of our council and other jurisdictions whatsoever of these our Realms that they keep, fulfill and execute, and cause to be kept, fulfilled and executed this our permit and all things granted therein. Given at San Lorenzo [del Escorial] on the twenty-ninth day of the month of June, one thousand, five hundred and seventy-five years.

      I, the King
By order of His Majesty   Antonio de Erasso

Fol. II: Dedication

To the very illustrious sir, the learned Hernando de Hábalos de Sotomayor of the Supreme council; Esteban Daza, your servant, peace, happiness, and health⁷ desires:

Victurus liber debet habere genium, the book which has lasting value (most illustrious sir), says Marcial, has to have wit. I wish then with the same love which every father has toward his sons, that even if they be ugly and idle, desiring that this book of mine may survive and live for many years, I knew not to which wit to whom better I might be able to give it, than to your grace, whose eminence in letters, worth of person, splendor of life, and integrity of manners are such that no greater protection against jealous tongues, nor surer favor and aid amongst the good, will this my book be able to take, than to have the name of your grace written and stamped on its brow. And as it, and its author, have sought the support of such a lord, offense would your grace do to deny your protection to one who, with the humility of a true servant, takes refuge under your care, as the best and safest that virtuous labor can have in these days in Spain. And considering that services of this quality merit to be esteemed, more for the good will with which they are offered than for their worth, may you, not despising the poverty of the present work, use my good will and person, as of one most obliged whenever, for things of greater import, such should be of service to your grace whose most illustrious person and station may Our Lord, etc.

Fol. II[v]: Epigram

Dialogue concerning Stephen Dazza, between Apollo and the Muses.

Wherefore, father, art thou happier than usual? Phoebus, having slain the python, you scarcely rejoice so much in your own radiance, as [in the fact] that now, O God, with all your divine strength you consider Dazza worthy of your cithara and songs.

In this, indeed, I rejoice. You, Muses, likewise rejoice. May his lyre so extol your honor that it becomes for him a truthful foreteller [= pledge] of eternity, that he may dwell in heaven with greater joy.

All the difficult and easy fantasias are shown with two letters at the beginning, that is, with the letter D and the letter F, which means that those with the letter D are difficult and those with the letter F are *facil* [easy].

Fols. iii, iii^v, iv: Explanation of the Tablature

Short and condensed rule to understand these ciphers and some of their beauties, so that with which rule, knowing how to sing a little from mensural notation, one can easily apply it to the vihuela, and understand some of the doubts which may occur by not having laws by which to know them. And I will always be as short as possible, because I cannot say much that others have not already dealt with.

The six long lines represent the six strings of the vihuela taking them in this manner:

- sixth ―――
- fifth ―――
- fourth ―――
- third ―――
- second ―――
- first ―――

The figures represent numbers, counting from one to ten. Example, 1, 2, 3, 4, 5, 6, 7, 8, 9, X, except the figure 0 which, upon the string it falls, has to be played open.

All these numbers show upon which fret one has to play the strings, and so the number 1, on the string which it falls, has to be played on the first fret, and so the number 2 is played on the second fret, and consequently with the remainder. And all the numbers which might be above one another are played together on the strings on which they fall, and when they are apart from one another, each is played on its own. Example:[8]

The figures of mensural notation which are above the lines show the [rhythmic] value of the *golpes* [strokes],[9] and so each number that is with others or on its own is given the value of the figure which it has as its sign. Example [see below]:

The dots which are found in the spaces between one line and another serve to guide the numbers which have to be played together; and also serve to guide the figures of mensural notation above the numbers which they have to be, as appears in the example which I gave above.

The lines which cross the strings divide the measures, which are all the strokes that are from one line to the next. If it is one stroke, it will be given the value of a *semibrevis*; if there are two strokes, each will be given the value of a *minima*; if there are four strokes, they will be given the value of four *seminimas*; and if there are eight strokes, they will be given the value of eight *corcheas*; so that each number of these four sizes makes a *compasillo* [measure].[10] Example:

All of the strokes which may have one rhythmic figure or another are played to the *compás* [beat], and they will be given the value of the figure which is above them: that if one stroke is a *semibrevis*, all the following strokes will each be worth a *semibrevis* until arriving at another figure; and if it were the figure of a *minima*, each stroke would be worth a *minima*; and consequently one will play each stroke as if it were the figure of which it takes its value, as can clearly be seen in the previous example.

We have already dealt with the understanding of the strings, frets, figures, and of the manner in which they have to be played, observing the order in which we have spoken. It remains to deal with the *compás* [tactus]. *Compás* is the name for the distance or space which one counts with the foot or with the hand, which is from one beat [*golpe*] to the next: and so there are two types of *compás*: major and minor. The major comprises two of the minor, which is called *compasillo* with which this book deals; and it is more common by being easier and clearer to understand, because all that one sings is *compasillo*, which is the value of a semibrevis, two *minimas*, four *seminimas*, or eight *corcheas*, any of which makes a *compasillo*, which is the value of a *semibrevis*, two *minimas*, four *seminimas*, or eight *corcheas*, any of which makes a *compasillo*. Example:

I shall not deal with proportions, for in this book one will not find any species of proportion.

Fols. iv-iv^v: List of Errata
Fols. 114^v-115^v: Table of Contents
Fol. 116: Colophon

The present book, made by Esteban Daza, was printed in the most noble town of Valladolid by Diego Fernández de Córdoba, printer to His Majesty, and was finished on the twelfth day of April in the year 1576.

Fol. 1: Title page of the *libro primero*

Comiença el libro primero, el qual/trata de muchas Fantasias de Esteuan Daça,/ a tres y a quatro. Van al principio los ocho tonos a quatro, por su or-/den, y despues van otras fantasias por differentes tonos, y en to-/das las de a quatro va señalada la voz del Tenor con / vnos puntillos, para que si quisieren la can-/ten: y las de a tres va señalada la / voz de Contra alto.

(Here begins the first book containing many fantasias by Esteban Daza *a 3* and *a 4*. First come the eight modes *a 4*, in their order, and after come other fantasias in different modes, and in all those *a 4*, the tenor voice is indicated by *puntillos*, so that they can be sung if desired, and those *a 3* have the altus indicated.)

The *libro primero* is a systematically organized collection of pieces. The fantasias are in four groups. Fantasias 1–8 are in four voices and arranged in order of mode as stated above. Numbers 9–12 are in three voices, nos. 13–18 are in four voices, and nos. 19–22 are *de passos largos para desemuolver las manos* (in long figural passages to develop the hands). Eleven works, nos. 3, 7, 9–14, 16–18, are indicated in the source as being "easy"; the other eleven are indicated as "difficult." With the exception of the final group of fantasias, nos. 19–22, all works have a rubric to indicate mode and theoretical tuning. Additional indications show that fantasias 14–16 are in transposed modes. These rubrics are reproduced in the tablature in this edition (see pp. 47-81), and they are translated into English in the Critical Notes.

The *puntillos* (see translation of the title page above), used to indicate either the tenor or alto voice in the first eighteen works, are oblique slashes at the top right-hand side of the relevant tablature figures. Irrespective of whether one chooses to sing these lines or not, the *puntillos* facilitate the task of distinguishing the independent voices of the texture equally for performance or editorial purposes. All the fantasias have the same mensural sign, ₵, indicating *compasillo*.

The printing style of *El Parnasso* is austere and accurate. Decoration in the book is limited to the ornamental borders of the title pages, the illuminated letters beginning each section of the prefatory texts, and an engraving of a mythological figure with the monogram 'CR' at its feet that appears at the end of *libro tercero* (fol. 114). The same vignette is found beneath the colophon in the vihuela book *Silva de Sirenas* (1547) of Enriquez de Valderrábano, and in Tomás de Santa María's treatise, the *Arte de Tañer Fantasía* (1565), lib. 1, fol. 90ᵛ.[11] These books, and Narváez's *Los seys libros del Delphín* (1538), all emanated from the Fernández de Córdoba presses in Valladolid. The price of 136 *maravedís* printed in the Munich exemplar of *El Parnasso* (130 in the Madrid copy) in the year of publication was the sum required to purchase 11.5 liters of milk, 12.6 liters of wine, or seven quires of writing paper.[12]

The Music

Daza's Treatment of the Fantasia

Either as a formal archetype or a compositional process, the sixteenth-century instrumental fantasia defies precise definition. Because they have so many individual differences, Spanish fantasias of the period can only loosely be defined as abstract compositions that have no particular textual or performance function; they are composed polyphonically and are of no fixed length or formal design. Spanish fantasias of this period are generally non-repetitive, and derive from an improvisatory tradition of simultaneous composition and performance.

Daza's music, although original and imaginative, is conservative and reflects no desire on the part of the composer to venture into previously unexplored territory.[13] Daza competently maneuvered his inspiration within an established style, imbuing that style with his own personality.

In conceiving his fantasias, Daza made use of two styles: one employs the imitative techniques found particularly in sixteenth-century motets; and the other uses procedures inspired by the idiomatic potential of his chosen instrument. Fantasias 1–18 are entirely dominated by imitative motet procedures; nos. 19–22 are constructed with sections of idiomatic vihuela writing that alternate with sections of imitation. As he adapted motet procedures to his fantasias, Daza firmly adhered to the well-established precepts of imitative contrapuntal writing and to the central aesthetic of equal-voiced polyphony. However, he diverged from motet style in that he compressed the overall length and used shorter themes than are typically found in sixteenth-century motets. This was Daza's response to his awareness of the difficulty of sustaining involved contrapuntal textures on the vihuela for long periods, and he succeeded in altering this aspect of the motet style without compromising the total effect. Daza's second style in these vihuela pieces is characterized by the utilization of the instrument's inherent idiomatic resources. The composer wrote long scale passages, often as sequences, and he frequently divided the texture into unequal parts, with one voice predominating over the others. For example, in many passages, one voice dominates by playing rapid figures, while the other voices band together into a less active accompaniment.

Although Daza's writing is basically conservative, these works do deviate markedly from the earlier tradition of improvisatory fantasias. The pieces in this edition reflect a desire to refine and condense improvisatory and spontaneous elements. Daza's compositions, at least in the form in which they were published, appear far from improvised. They are refined and balanced, and many of them exhibit characteristics of deliberate formal design. These works are instrumental motets rather than pure improvisatory musical fantasy.

The Compositional Process

Examination of the musical substance of Daza's fantasias reveals regular patterns of voice leading, consistent treatment of minor aspects of counterpoint, and constant attention to detail in all respects. So thorough is the attention to detail, and so rigorous is the approach to counterpoint, that one cannot escape the hypothesis that, in addition to not being improvised, the eighteen imitative fantasias in the *libro primero* of *El Parnasso* were not composed directly onto the vihuela. Rather, they were conceived intellectually, with instrumental limitations kept in mind; perhaps they were first notated mensurally, and then transferred onto the vihuela by the same process used in intabulating a motet or madrigal. This hypothesis hinges on the fact that the tuning rubrics (see Critical Notes for translations) found in the source at the beginning of Fantasias 1–18 are linked to intabulation procedures. After conceiving or composing each work, Daza had to determine the most suitable way of fitting the music onto the vihuela. He used the procedures that were practiced by other vihuelists and that were carefully explained by the theorist Juan Bermudo.[14] Had Daza worked directly onto the instrument, his music would surely reflect a style more closely dictated by instrumental limitations and possibilities.

The vihuela, like the lute and viol, was tuned to the intervals of a 4th, 4th, major 3rd, 4th, 4th, above the pitch of the lowest course. Bermudo described the vihuela with G as its lowest pitch as the usual instrument, the *vihuela común*, and it is evident from the transcriptions of the fantasias by Daza that are without tuning rubrics (nos. 19–22) that he thought of these pieces as being in this common tuning. However, practical advice given by Luis Milán in the preface of *El Maestro* qualified Bermudo's description: in giving advice concerning the selection of vihuela strings, Milán recommended that the player find an accurately made thin string for the first course, tune it as high as it would go, and then tune the lower strings from it.[15] Thus, the instrument was actually tuned to an arbitrarily determined pitch; according to Bermudo, however, it was *imagined* to be tuned in G.

The vihuelists from Narváez onward thought of their instrument not only in terms of the *vihuela común* tuning, but also in terms of a number of other imaginary tunings that were equally unrelated to the real sound of the instrument. With such imaginary tunings, the lowest string could be considered to be tuned to virtually any pitch. The purpose of these imaginary tunings was to facilitate the intabulation of vocal works. Bermudo counseled his readers to examine the compass and mode of a work and to select the imaginary tuning that would render the work most playable. As an aid to the intabulator, Bermudo provided fingerboard diagrams for seven imaginary tunings, including the common G tuning.[16] Each of these fingerboard diagrams also shows how the movable frets of the instrument should be altered in order to preserve the intervalic relationship of the quasi-Pythagorean temperament in which Spanish instruments were tuned.

Daza applied to his fantasias the same principles of intabulation described by Bermudo. The root notes of the final chords of seventeen of the twenty-two fantasias in this edition are placed on the open fourth, fifth, or sixth courses. The remaining five works all end on the second fret of those courses.[17] The application of these intabulation principles facilitates performance, because it results in settings that frequently use open strings and employ chord configurations typical of lute and vihuela writing. The four idiomatic fantasias without tuning rubrics, nos. 19–22 in this edition, are transcribed here in the G-tuning of the *vihuela común*. Numbers 21 and 22 result in their proper modes, while nos. 19 and 20 reveal the common practice of the First mode transposed to G. Thus, it appears more likely that these idiomatic pieces were composed with instrument in hand.

Daza was not the only vihuelist to use tuning rubrics for fantasias. He probably derived the practice from Narváez, who included similar rubrics for all his fantasias. Moreover, as has been shown above, Daza modeled the preface of *El Parnasso* on that written by Narváez. Pisador included tuning rubrics for his ostinato fantasias, all of which use a *cantus prius factus*. Mudarra, Valderrábano, and Fuenllana also tacitly applied the same principles to their fantasias. That other vihuelists also employed the flexible system of using tunings based on imagined pitches for fantasias does not diminish the argument concerning Daza; rather, it suggests that these composers, too, may not have always worked directly onto the instrument. However, none of them made so few idiomatic concessions as Daza, nor does any of their music display such a thorough and rigorous technical approach as his does. Further, Daza's fantasias are conceived on a vastly different aesthetic plane that is just one step away from the extension of fantasia into fugue. His textures are detailed and complex, surely not improvisatory, For Fantasias 1–18, a four-stage creative process can be projected: (1) intellectual conception (with instrumental considerations); (2) notation in mensural form; (3) intabulation; (4) performance. Modification of the intial concept of a given piece could have occurred at any subsequent stage, and stage two could possibly have been circumvented, depending upon Daza's personal intellectual ability, about which we have no knowledge.

In form, Daza's fantasias consist of from three to seven successive independent episodes. With the exception of the idiomatic passages of nos. 19–22, each episode employs some type of imitative treatment of a single theme.[18] Thus, these works are non-repetitive, cumulative structures. Daza's customary technique within each episode was to introduce a theme once in each voice and then dismiss it by means of a standardized cadence. Occasionally he exposed his material twice, but he tended to avoid any involved musical argument. Less frequently, an additional entry of an imitative theme occurs in a brief non-imitative passage, and this usually results in a quasi-*cantus firmus* texture. The most common technique of voice entry used is paired imitation.[19] However, the third and fourth voices, forming the second *duo*, frequently enter later and later after each preceding entry, creating the effect of an expanding texture rather than the block contrasts of register that result from the use of repeated identical *duos* at the octave. In the openings of six fantasias, the theme of the *duos* have tonal answers.[20]

The themes employed in the fantasias are simple, formulaic, and not of great individual character.

The process by which they are woven into the contrapuntal fabric overshadows thematic individuality as a compositional priority. It is convenient and useful to divide Daza's themes into imitative "head-motives" and freely composed "tails." The head-motives are of fixed shape in all voices and provide the central imitative interplay of the compositions. The tails are different in each voice, and they fill the gap between head-motive and cadence, at the same time keeping the texture alive and on-going. Because of their repetition as fixed entities, the head-motives are the only part of the melodic material that can strictly be classified as "thematic." This manner of construction, with head-motives and tails, is both practical and musically effective: it emphasizes the entry of each voice, and it allows tails to be constructed that accommodate and enhance further head-motive entries. Thus, Daza's approach to plucked instrumental texture is a realistic one that allows all entries to be heard, while avoiding many potential performance difficulties. This texture allows both performer and listener to focus on the most salient events in the progress of the music. The head-motives are generally short (most are between one and three measures in length), and they usually move by step or by small leaps that only infrequently exceed a fifth. Except at the beginning of the fantasias, where Daza's melodies usually begin with a stately *semibrevis* (a half-note in the transcription), most themes begin on weak beats so that the exposed position and rhythmic impetus of their initial notes allows them to assert themselves with some presence. The second note of Daza's themes most commonly either repeats the first note or moves away from it by step. In those themes where this does not occur, the second note may move away from the first at a third, or at a fourth or fifth in an implied dominant-tonic function. In the few works with a double exposition of the first theme, the value of the customary opening *semibrevis* is usually halved for the second exposition.[21] Other methods of modifying themes are used only infrequently. For example, inversion occurs only in the rapid scale passages of the idiomatic fantasia group[22]; and thematic transformation occurs in a few works, such as no. 11, where themes 5 (mm. 19–26) and 7 (mm. 31–37) appear to be derived from theme 4 (mm. 14–19):

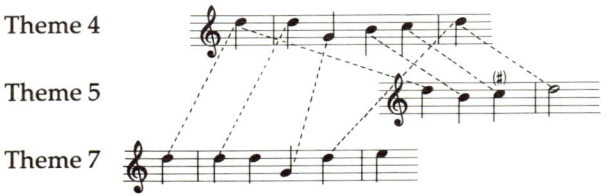

Rhythmically, Daza's themes are simple, although there are several instances of themes being placed to disrupt metric uniformity. Theme 3 of Fantasia 17 (mm. 21–32) is a typical example.

Free, non-imitative counterpoint does not abound in these works, except for the *passos largos* of nos. 19–22. Several works, for example nos. 5, 12, and 21, have short codas of four or five measures in length, and elements of these codas can usually be related to previous parts of each work. Few of the imitative works have free internal episodes: apart from some latitude at cadences, it is difficult to find places where there is no closely controlled thematic activity.

Daza employed a number of cadential formulae to terminate episodes, and these endings occur with the same predictability as the cadences of eighteenth-century recitatives. The formula that appears most often in the fantasias is a V-I progression, with an unembellished 4-3 suspension over the dominant, or frequently with the uppermost voice ornamented, using either of the following *redoble* formulae:

Progressions of VII$^6_3$-I are often used as final cadences, as are unresolved reiterations of dominant chords. Several of the varieties of interrupted cadence common in sixteenth-century style are also to be found. Occasionally, a descending octave scale figure immediately follows the resolution of a cadence, generally in places where the previous passage had gained considerable momentum.

Although the fantasias are made up of independent episodes, there is a strong sense of unity within each piece. Basic cohesion is provided by the primary musical elements of meter, rhythm, melodic range, counterpoint, harmony, and modality/tonality. Each of the first eighteen fantasias is quite consistent and homogeneous. The episodes of nos. 19–22, however, are marked by contrast rather than by homogeneity. In several works, particular intervals or rhythmic patterns form themselves into motivic cells and permeate all or several of the episodes. Such motivic material occurs in all voices, but it is usually reserved for those times when the part is not stating the theme. Deeper examination of the fantasias reveals a more structured unity. Regardless of whether formal balance was consciously or intuitively achieved by Daza, patterns occur in these works in several areas, including thematic shape, tonal progression, and voice entries. A few examples that suggest a concern with unity of the outer formal structure are the contrasting alternation of themes in no. 2; the regular sectional alternation of voice-leading patterns in no. 9; the presence of a common theme at the beginning and end of no. 9; the two consecutive groups of three related themes in no. 11; the ratio of section length (2:1:2:1) of no. 14; and the division of no. 15 into three dramatic units of almost equal length (mm. 1–13, 13–26; 27–42).[23]

Daza's use of mode is indicative of the essentially conservative nature of his fantasias. He firmly abides by the rules governing finals, range, and cadence as expounded by early- and mid-sixteenth-century theorists.[24] He shows a typical sixteenth-century preference for mode 1. Several fantasias, nos. 1, 9, 13, 14, 18, 19, and 20, are in this mode. Modes 5 and 8 are each used three times, only one piece is in mode 3, and the remaining four modes are each used twice.

Editorial Methods

There are many ways in which old instrumental tablatures can be translated into modern musical language. This edition has been prepared in an attempt to restate faithfully the composer's musical ideas in the clearest and most consistent manner possible. The following principles have been applied. (1) The transcription reconstructs the polyphony implicit in the tablature. (2) Rhythmic values of the tablature are reduced 2:1 in the transcription. (3) The number of barlines in the tablature has been halved in the transcription, and thus the transcribed measure has the equivalence of twice the *tactus*. (4) For nos. 1–18, the pitch indications given in the rubrics of the source are applied to the transcription. Numbers 19–22 are all transcribed in G. The tuning is indicated at the head of each transcription. Each "imaginary vihuela" (see above) is tuned to the intervals 4th, 4th, major 3rd, 4th, 4th, above the pitch given as the tuning pitch. The tablature presented in diplomatic facsimile in this edition shows how the pieces can be realized on any vihuela at any pitch. (5) Only the *musica ficta* given in the source has been applied in the edition. A few accidentals have been added in parentheses by the editor as cautionary warnings. (6) Corrections, including those from Daza's errata, are incorporated into the tablature and the two-stave transcription and listed in the Critical Notes. (7) The *puntillos*, used in the tablature to indicate inner voices, are reproduced in the diplomatic facsimile. They mark the figures that form the tenor voice in nos. 1–8 and 13–18 and that form the altus in nos. 9–12. Editorial changes in the original placing of *puntillos* have been based on the logic of the voice-leading used by Daza; these changes are documented in the Critical Notes. (8) Daza's own consistent editorial methods as an intabulator of vocal works provide the basis for the following editorial policies in the present transcriptions: (a) making the half-note the longest duration in the transcription, with several exceptions; (b) transcribing one tablature figure as a unison between two voices in many instances; (c) generally preceding thematic voice entries with a quarter-rest.

The Munich exemplar of *El Parnasso* is the primary source for this edition. The titles above the works in both the transcription and the tablature are taken from the table of contents of *El Parnasso*. The edition maintains the original order of the works. It is hoped the separate tablature will facilitate performance and permit easy comparison with the two-stave transcription.

Performance Notes

The brevity of Daza's explanation of tablature and music "because I cannot say much that others have not already dealt with" (fol. iii) is an opportune invitation to relate what his contemporaries wrote about the areas of performance practice left unspecified by him.

Tempo

Choice of tempo appears to be related to manual dexterity within a limited range. Vihuelists Fuenllana and Pisador recommended that a *compás* (=*tactus*) be established in accordance with the player's technical ability, although Fuenllana stated that extremes of tempo, both fast and slow, are undesirable.[25] Most of the sixteenth-century Spanish writers on the subject either imply or state directly that the *tactus* should be maintained once the tempo is established.[26] A specific exception to this practice was made by Luis Milán as he referred to his works of alternating *consonancia* and *redoble* sections; he advocated slow performance of the homophonic *consonancias* and fast execution of the scale passages (*redobles*).[27] Later sixteenth-century sources neither confirm nor deny that this approach to tempo is valid for Daza's *fantasias de passos largos*. The vihuela books of Pisador, Fuenllana, and Daza do not have the tempo symbols or verbal tempo indications found in all the books published before 1550.[28]

xiv

Ornamentation

The southern European passion for embellishment is verified by the number of sixteenth-century manuals and treatises on the subject. Ornamentation following the examples of authors such as Ganassi and Ortiz is appropriate to the music of Daza. Except in sections of *passos largos,* Daza restricts his ornamentation largely to cadential areas and occasionally to sections of two-voice writing. The infrequency of other embellishment by no means precludes ornamentation; but it might well indicate a sympathy Daza shared with Bermudo, who offered the following advice to novices on the vihuela:

> He who wishes to profit from this book should take [this] as principal advice: don't smother the music with embellishments. The greatest corruption and waste of music that I find among players is importune embellishment.[29]

The implication is that ornamentation should not impede, disrupt, or hide the counterpoint in any way.[30]

Instrumentation

The fantasias in this volume need not be limited to performance on the vihuela. Lute and vihuela music are obviously interchangeable, and sixteenth-century practice makes keyboard instruments or harp legitimate substitutes as well. Indeed the specific titles of Hernando de Cabezón's edition of his father's works (*Obras,* 1578), and the anthology of Luis Venegas de Henestrosa (*Libro de cifra nueva,* 1557), both sub-titled "*para tecla, harpa y vihuela,*" indicate that any polyphonic instrument could be substituted for any other.

Critical Notes

The following information is provided for each piece: the folio number in *El Parnasso,* an English translation of the rubric (for those pieces that have them), a translation of the table of contents entry in cases where it provides additional information, the tuning used in the transcription, and a list of discrepancies between this edition and the primary source (Valladolid, 1576; Bayerische Staatsbibliothek, Munich). Measure references are to the tablature; they are followed by a parenthetical citation of the corresponding transcription measure numbers. The numbers 1 and 2, separated by a point from the measure reference, specify *minima-*position in the tablature measure; similarly, the numbers 1–4 designate quarter-note-position in the transcription measures. For example, the second chord of tablature measure twenty of Fantasia 1 would be cited as "m. 20.2," followed by its equivalent in the transcription, given as "(m. 10.4)." Because 2:1 reduction is used in this edition, the original note value of the *minima* ↓ is equivalent to a quarter-note in the transcription, and the *semiminima* ↓ is equivalent to an eighth-note. Asterisks (*) indicate those corrections made in accordance with the list of errata in *El Parnasso,* itself.

[1.] Fantasia por el primer tono

Location: fols. 1-2ᵛ. Rubric: "The f'-clef is located on the second course at the first fret. Difficult." Table of contents: "Fantasia in the first mode." Tuning in A.

M.31.1 (m.16.1), rhythmic symbol is *minima,* corrected to *semiminima**; the note is blackened by hand in the Munich exemplar. M.38.2 (m.19.4), rhythmic symbol is *semiminima*; corrected to *minima*; altered by hand in the Munich exemplar. M.78.1 (m.39.3), a *puntillo* has been added.

[2.] Fantasia por el segundo tono

Location: fols. 2ᵛ-4. Rubric: "Fantasia in the second mode. The f'-clef [*sic* = f] is located on the fifth course at the third fret. Difficult." Tuning in A.

M.36.2 (m.18.4), a *puntillo* has been added to fret numeral 1 on course 3.

[3.] Fantasia por el tercero tono

Location: fols. 4-6. Rubric: "Fantasia in the third mode. The f-clef is located on the fifth course at the third fret. Easy." Tuning in A.

[4.] Fantasia por el quarto tono

Location: fols. 6-7. Rubric: "Fantasia in the fourth mode. The f-clef is located on the fourth course at the first fret. Difficult." Tuning in F♯.

M.70.2 (m.35.2), a *puntillo* has been omitted and the figure reassigned in this edition to the altus. M.80.2 (m.40.2), *semiminima* is over fret numeral 5 of course 1 instead of over fret numeral 3 of course 2.*

[5.] Fantasia por el quinto tono

Location: fols. 7-8ᵛ. Rubric: "Fantasia in the fifth mode. The f'-clef [*sic* = f] is located on the open fourth course. Difficult." Tuning in G.

M.7.2 (m.4.2), a *puntillo* has been added. M.41.2 (m.21.2), a *puntillo* has been added. M.84.1 (m.42.3), a *puntillo* has been omitted from fret numeral 0 on course 5.

[6.] Fantasia por el sexto tono

Location: fols. 8ᵛ-10. Rubric: "Fantasia in the

sixth mode. The f-clef is located on the fourth course at the second fret. Difficult." Tuning in F.

M.21.1 (m.11.1), *minima* is added*; Munich exemplar emended by hand.

[7.] Fantasia por el septimo tono

Location: fols. 10-11. Rubric: "Fantasia in the seventh mode. The f-clef is located on the fifth course at the third fret. Easy." Tuning in A.

[8.] Fantasia por el octauo tono

Location: fols. 11-12ᵛ. Rubric: "Fantasia in the eighth mode. The c'-clef is located on the third course at the third fret. Difficult." Tuning in G.

[9.] Fantasia a tres, por el primer tono

Location: fols. 12ᵛ-14. Rubric: "Following are several fantasias *a 3*, in which the middle voice, the altus, is indicated with *puntillos*, and this first one in the first mode has the f'-clef [*sic* = f?] located on the third course at the first fret. Easy." Tuning in D.

M.26.1 (m.13.3), a *puntillo* has been added.

[10.] Fantasia a tres, por el quinto tono

Location: fols. 14-15. Rubric: "Fantasia in the fifth mode *a 3*. The f-clef is located on the open fourth course. Easy." Tuning in G.

[11.] Fantasia a tres, por el septimo tono

Location: fols. 15ᵛ-16ᵛ. Rubric: "Fantasia in the seventh mode, *a 3*. The f-clef is located on the fifth course at the third fret. Easy." Tuning in A.

M. 26 (m.13.1-2), the rhythmic signs *minima, semiminima* are reversed to *semiminima, minima*. M.69.2 (m.34.4), the second fret numeral 3 of course 3 in this measure is printed over the second *semiminima* value rather than the third*.

[12.] Fantasia a tres, por el octauo tono

Location: fols. 16ᵛ-18. Rubric: "Fantasia *a 3* in the eighth mode. The f-clef is located on the open fourth course. Easy." Tuning in G.

[13.] Fantasia por el primer tono

Location: fols. 18ᵛ-19ᵛ. Rubric: "Fantasia in the first mode, *a 4*. The f-clef is located on the open fourth course, and the tenor voice is indicated with *puntillos*, as is done in all those which follow. Easy." Tuning in G.

M.50.2 (m.25.2), a *puntillo* has been added.

[14.] Fanta[sia] por el pri[mer] tono, por gesolreut

Location: fols. 20-21ᵛ. Rubric: "Fantasia in the first mode transposed to G, *a 4*. The f-clef is located on the third course at the third fret. Easy." Tuning in C, transcribed an octave higher than indicated by the rubric.

M.75.2 (m.38.2), the rhythmic symbol is a *minima* instead of a *semiminima**.

[15.] Fa[n]ta[sia] por el segu[ndo] tono, por gesolreut

Location: fols. 21ᵛ-23. Rubric: "Fantasia in the second mode, *a 4*, transposed to G. The f-clef is located on the open fourth course, and the work contains some embellishment. Difficult." Tuning in G.

[16.] Fanta[sia] por [el] quarto tono, por alamire

Location: fols. 23-24ᵛ. Rubric: "Fantasia *a 4* in the fourth mode, transposed to A. The f-clef is located on the open fourth course. Easy." Tuning in G.

M.20.2 (m.10.2), a *puntillo* has been omitted and the figure reassigned to the altus, not tenor. M.22 (m.11.1-2), the *semiminima* is placed at the beginning of the measure*. M.74.1 (m.37.1), the rhythmic symbol of a *minima* appears above fret numeral 2 of course 2 in the source. M.77.2 (m.38.4), fret numeral 2 on course 2 is printed as 3 in the source; i.e., the alto voice is e rather than the source f.

[17.] Fantasia por el sexto tono

Location: fols. 24ᵛ-26. Rubric: "Fantasia in the sixth mode. The f-clef is located on the open fourth course. Easy." Tuning in G.

[18.] Fantasia por el primer tono

Location: fols. 26-27. Rubric: "Fantasia in the first mode *a 4*. The f-clef is located on the third course at the first fret. Easy." Tuning in D.

[19.] Fantasia [de passos largos] por el primer tono

Location: fols. 27-29ᵛ. Rubric. "Following are some fantasias which contain several passages to develop the hands. Difficult." Table of contents: "Fantasia in the first mode." Tuning in G, rendering the mode transposed to G.

[20.] Fantasia [de passos largos] por el mismo [= primer] tono

Location: fols. 29ᵛ-31. Rubric: "Fantasia of long passages to develop the hands. Difficult." Table of contents: "Fantasia in the same mode, i.e., mode one." Tuning in G, rendering the mode transposed to G.

[21.] Fantasia [de passos largos] por el quinto tono

Location: fols. 31-33. Rubric: "Fantasia of long passages to develop the hands. Difficult." Table of contents: "Fantasia in the fifth mode." Tuning in G.

[22.] Fantasia [de passos largos] por el octauo tono

Location: fols. 33-34^v. Rubric: "Fantasia of long passages to develop the hands. Difficult." Table of contents: "Fantasia in the eighth mode." Tuning in G.

Acknowledgments

I take this opportunity to extend my gratitude to the Bayerische Staatsbibliothek, Munich, for providing a microfilm of the primary source of *El Parnasso*, and to the Lute Society of America, whose microfilm copies of so many other sources have greatly aided the preparation of this edition. I am also indebted to Professor Howard Mayer Brown of the University of Chicago for his many helpful suggestions concerning this edition.

May 1982

John Griffiths
University of Melbourne

Notes

1. Julio de Atienza, *Nobilario Español, Diccionario Heráldico de Apellidos Españoles y de Títulos Nobilarios* (Madrid, 1959), p. 333.
2. The six vihuela books printed before *El Parnasso* by Milán, Narváez, Mudarra, Valderrábano, Pisador, and Fuenllana, respectively, are described and inventoried and indexed as 1536[5], 1538[1], 1546[14], 1547[5], 1552[7], and 1554[3] in Howard Mayer Brown, *Instrumental Music Printed Before 1600, A Bibliography* (Cambridge, Mass., 1967).
3. The Lisbon copy of *El Parnasso*, unverified by Brown (*Instrumental Music*, p. 283), has been confirmed. This copy lacks the title page, the three preliminary folios, and the last folio; the penultimate folio is incomplete. It is catalogued RES. 376 P. The Biblioteca de San Lorenzo del Escorial, Spain, reports that it has no copy of *El Parnasso*, contrary to the assertion by Johannes Wolf in his *Handbuch der Notationskunde* (Leipzig, 1919), II:114.
4. *El Parnasso* is indexed as 1576[1] in Brown, *Instrumental Music*, pp. 281–283.
5. In the translation of this material here, these preliminary unnumbered folios are assigned lower-case Roman numerals in order to distinguish them from the Arabic numerals used to cite the numbered folios of the source.
6. Narváez's explanation is reproduced in his *Los seys libros del Delphín de Música de cifras para tañer Vihuela* (Valladolid, 1538), ed. Emilio Pujol, Monumentos de la Música Española, III (Barcelona, 1945; reprint, 1971): 19–21.
7. Given in the source as "P.F.y S.," which to all accounts is not a standard abbreviation; it is taken here as meaning *paz, felicidad y salud*.
8. The transcription of this example, and those following, is editorial. It is in the same 2:1 reduction that prevails in the transcriptions in the edition.
9. *Golpe*, translated as "stroke," is the term used to describe each time a note or chord is plucked.
10. The term *compasillo* is a diminutive of *compás*, which means "beat or "measure." As Daza explains in subsequent paragraphs, the *compasillo* measure has one down-beat and one up-beat, and is hence equivalent to a modern measure of $\frac{2}{4}$.
11. Pujol, in his edition of *Silva de Sirenas* by Enriquez de Valderrábano, Monumentos de la Música Española, XXII (Barcelona, 1965): 22, describes the figure as the god Mercury. His claim that the monogram was that of the printer cannot be supported, since the same engraving appears twice in Pisador's *Libro de musica de vihuela* (fols. viii^v, xvi^v), which was produced in identical type by the author himself in his home in Salamanca.
12. Earl J. Hamilton, *American Treasure and the Price Revolution in Spain, 1501–1650* (Cambridge, Mass., 1934), Appendices II, pp. 311–318, and IV, pp. 335–357.
13. John Ward, "The Vihuela de Mano and its Music (1536–1576)" (Ph.D. diss, New York University, 1953), pp. 272 ff. Ward concurs with this view in his discussion of Daza's fantasias; this discussion is based almost entirely on quotations from Santa María's treatise.
14. Juan Bermudo, *Declaración de Instrumentos Musicales* (Ossuna, 1555; facsimile reprint ed., Kassel, 1957), ed. Santiago Kastner, *Documenta Musicologia* XI. See fol. xc^v, and fols. xcviii^v-ci.
15. Luis Milán, *El Maestro* (1536), fol. Aiii^v. For an English translation, see Charles Jacobs's edition of *El Maestro* (University Park: Pennsylvania State University Press, 1971), p. 15.
16. Milán, *El Maestro*, diagrams appear on fols. cvi-cvii.
17. Nos. 3, 9, 13, 14, and 16.
18. Polythematic sections with theme and counter-theme occur in no. 1, mm. 31–36, and in no. 22, mm. 1–5.
19. Ward, "The Vihuela de Mano," pp. 272 ff., elaborates on Daza's use of this technique.
20. Nos. 6, 7, 8, 13, 16, and 17.
21. E.g., in nos. 3, 14, and 18. These note values are, respectively, half-notes and quarter-notes in the transcription.
22. E.g., in no. 19, opening measures.
23. The thematic resemblances of no. 2 are described in John Griffiths, "The Vihuela Book 'El Parnaso' by Esteban Daza," *Studies in Music* 10 (1976): 37-51. A more detailed discussion of the formal aspect of the fantasias will be presented in Griffiths, "The Vihuela Fantasia: A Comparative Study of Forms and Styles" (Ph.D diss., Monash University, in progress).
24. An adequate summary of these rules is found in P.

Samuel Rubio, *La Polifonía Clássica* (El Escorial, 1956).

25. Miguel de Fuenllana, *Orphénica Lyra* (Seville, 1554), prefatory fol. v; Pisador, *Libro de Música* (Salamanca, 1552), prefatory fol. iii.

26. *Tactus* was usually expressed as the raising and lowering of a hand or foot.

27. Milán, *El Maestro*, fol. D.

28. See Charles Jacobs, *Tempo Notation in Renaissance Spain* (Brooklyn, 1964) for a comprehensive study.

29. "Tenga por auiso principal el que deste libro sequisiere aprouechar: que en la musica no heche glosas. La mayor corrupcion y perdida de musica que entre tañedores hallo; es las importunas glosas." Bermudo, *Declaración*, fol. xxix[v].

30. Howard Mayer Brown, *Embellishing Sixteenth-Century Music*, Early Music Series 1, (London, 1976).

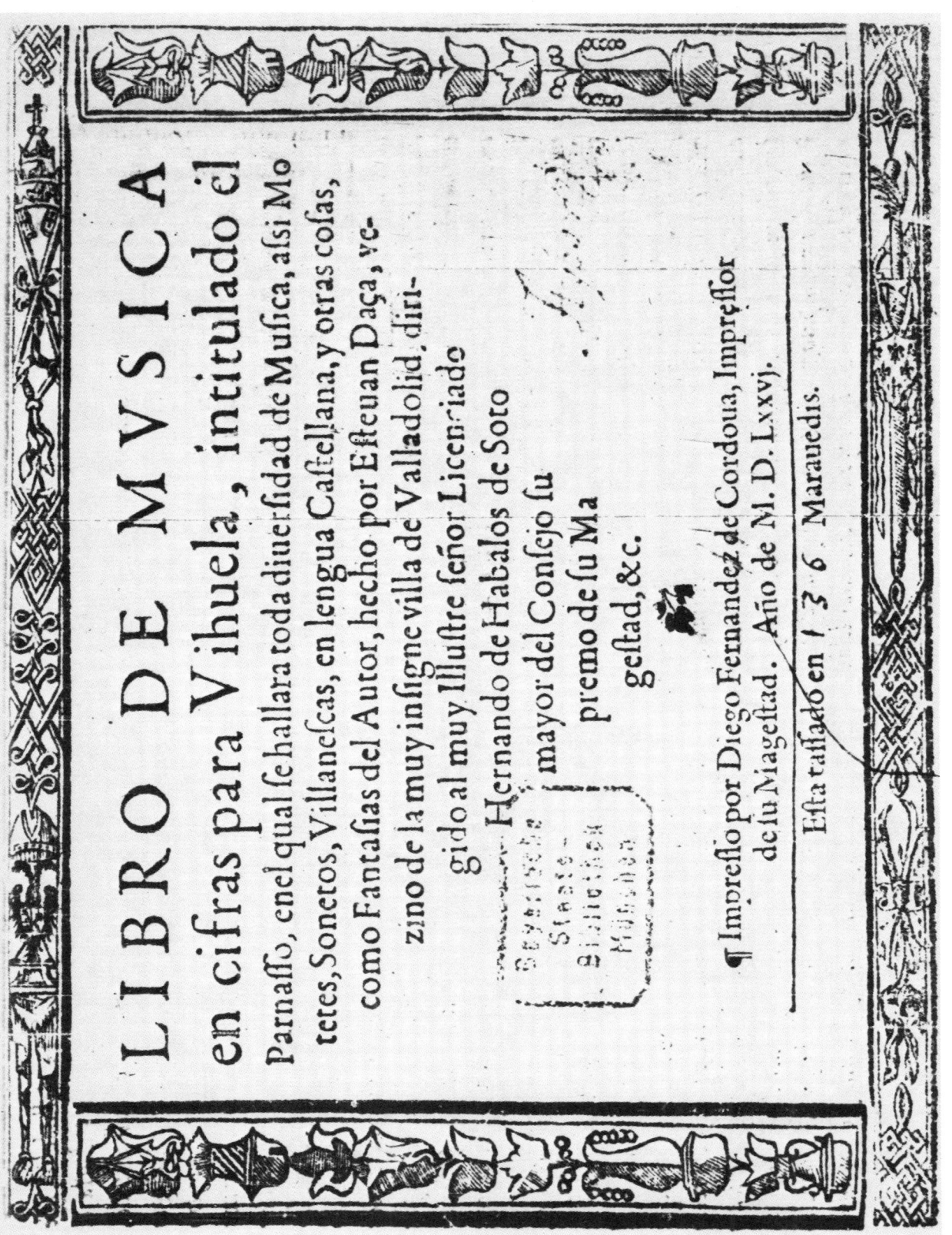

Plate I. Esteban Daza, *El Parnasso* (1576), title page. (Actual size, 205 x 145 mm.) (Bayerische Staatsbibliothek, Munich)

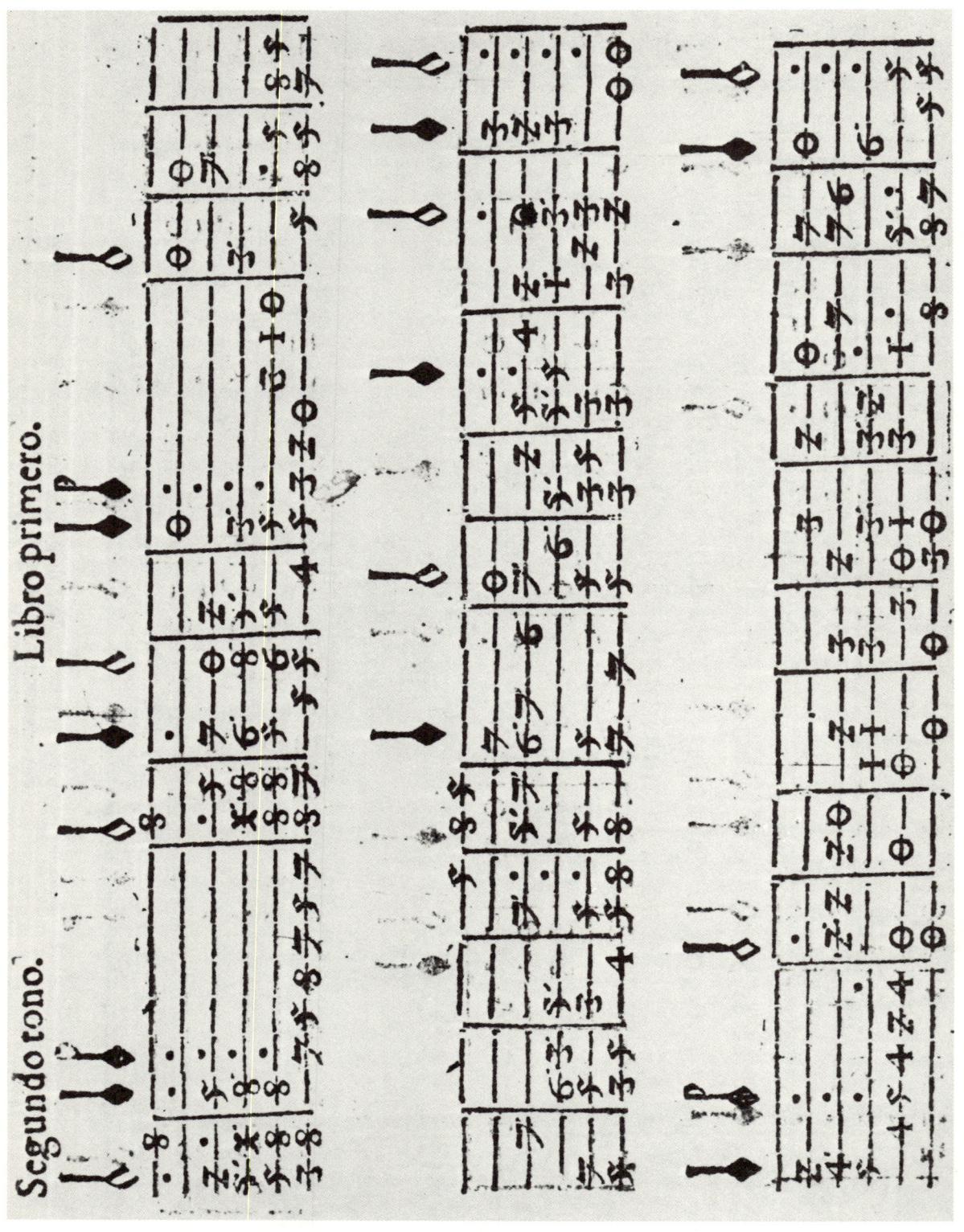

Plate II. Esteban Daza, *El Parnasso* (1576), *Fantasia por el segundo tono*, mm. 40–69, fol. 3ᵛ. (Actual size, 205 x 145 mm.) (Bayerische Staatsbibliothek, Munich)

THE FANTASIAS FOR VIHUELA
Two-stave Transcription

[1.] Fantasia por el primer tono

[Vihuela in A]

[2.] Fantasia por el segundo tono

[3.] Fantasia por el tercero tono

[Vihuela in A]

[4.] Fantasia por el quarto tono

[Vihuela in F#]

[5.] Fantasia por el quinto tono

[Vihuela in G]

[6.] Fantasia por el sexto tono

[Vihuela in F]

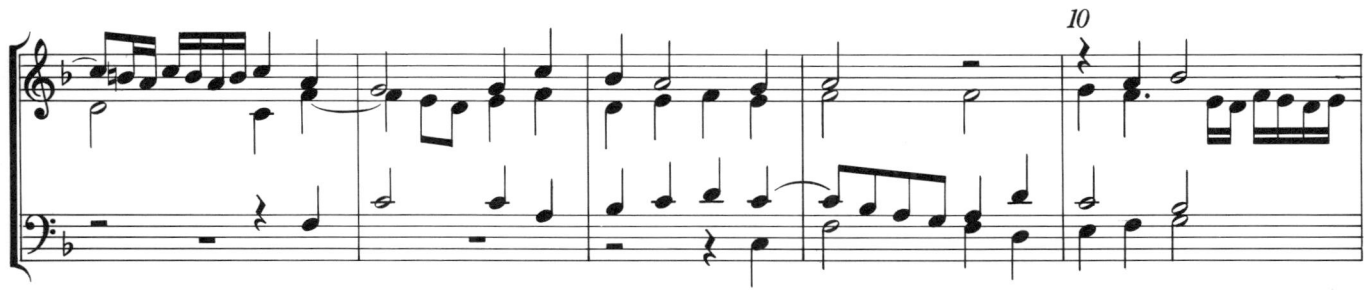

[7.] Fantasia por el septimo tono

[8.] Fantasia por el octauo tono

[Vihuela in G]

[9.] Fantasia a tres, por el primer tono

[Vihuela in D]

[10.] Fantasia a tres, por el quinto tono

[Vihuela in G]

[11.] Fantasia a tres, por el septimo tono

[Vihuela in A]

[12.] Fantasia a tres, por el octauo tono

[Vihuela in G]

[13.] Fantasia por el primer tono

[Vihuela in G]

[14.] Fanta[sia] por el pri[mer] tono, por gesolreut

[Vihuela in C]

[15.] Fa[n]ta[sia] por el segu[ndo] tono, por gesolreut

[Vihuela in G]

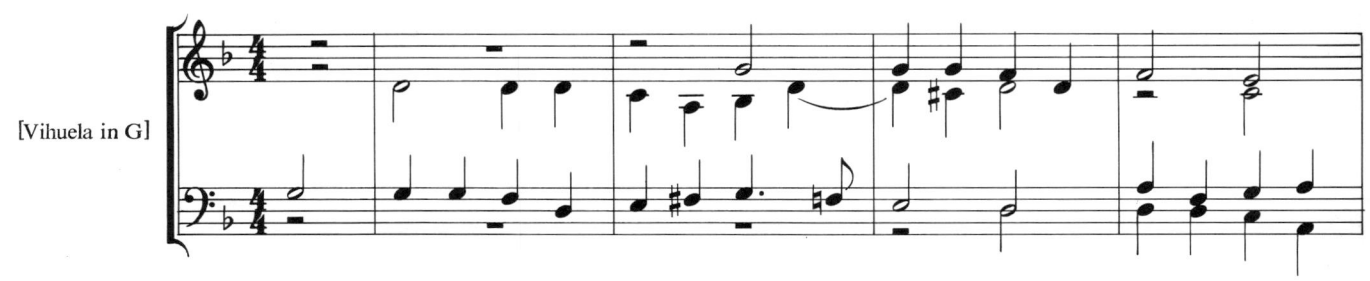

[16.] Fanta[sia] por [el] quarto tono, por alamire

[Vihuela in G]

[17.] Fantasia por el sexto tono

[Vihuela in G]

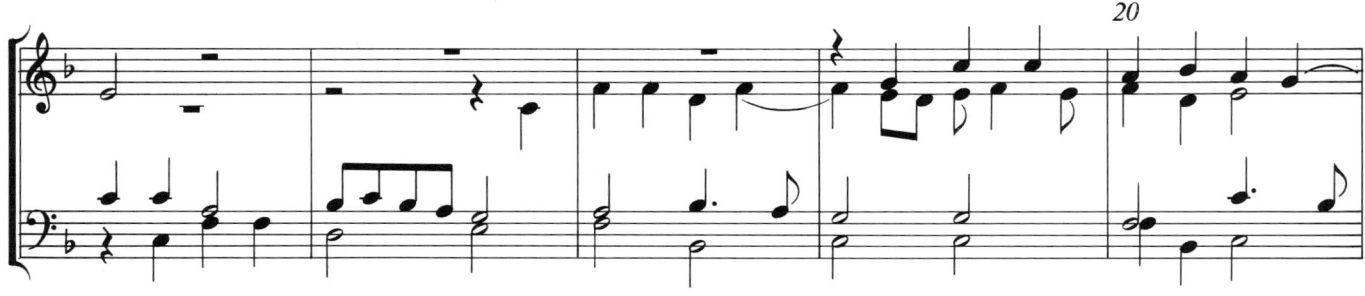

[18.] Fantasia por el primer tono

[19.] Fantasia [de passos largos] por el primer tono

[20.] Fantasia [de passos largos] por el mismo [=primer] tono

[Vihuela in G]

[21.] Fantasia [de passos largos] por el quinto tono

[Vihuela in G]

[22.] Fantasia [de passos largos] por el octauo tono

THE FANTASIAS FOR VIHUELA
Tablature

[1.] Fantasia por el primer tono

Señalase la claue de fefaut segunda en primero traste.

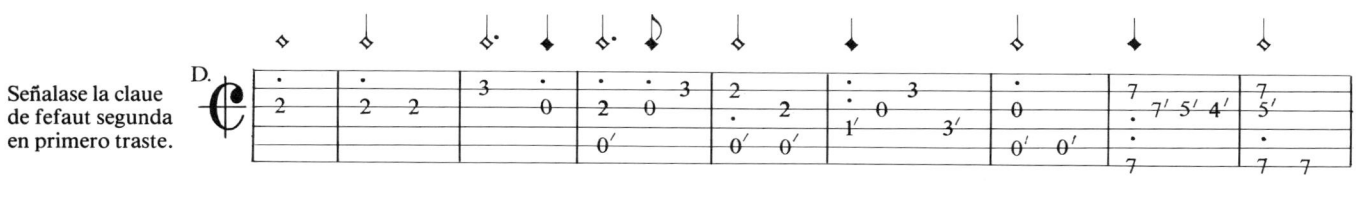
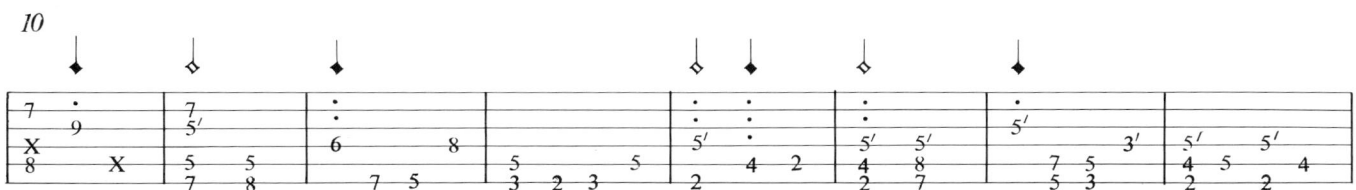
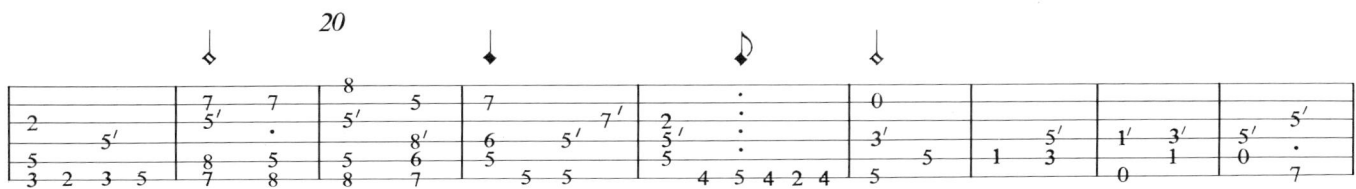
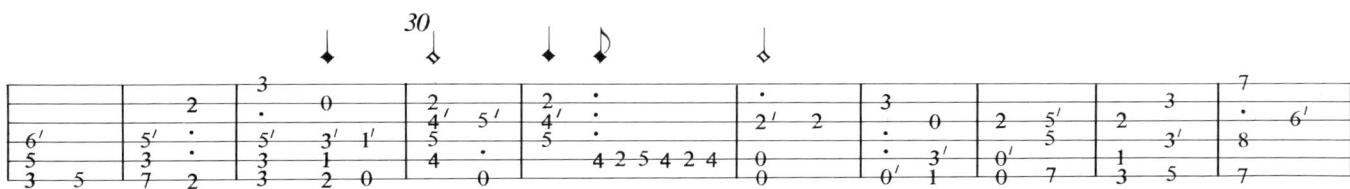
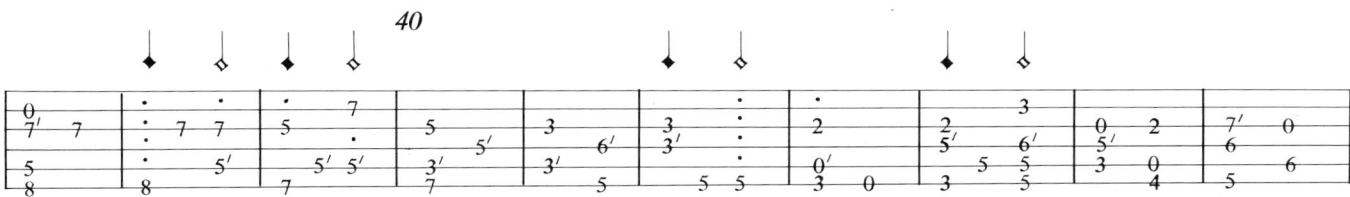
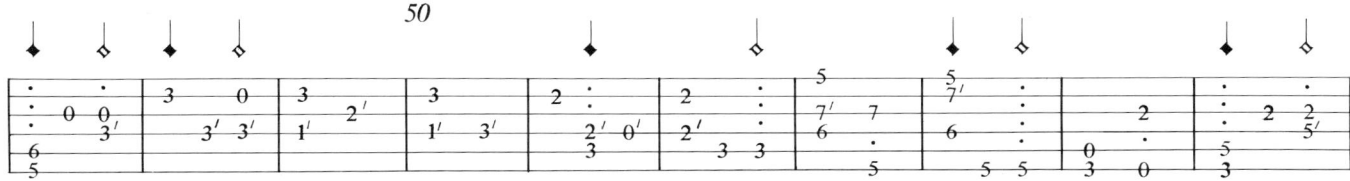

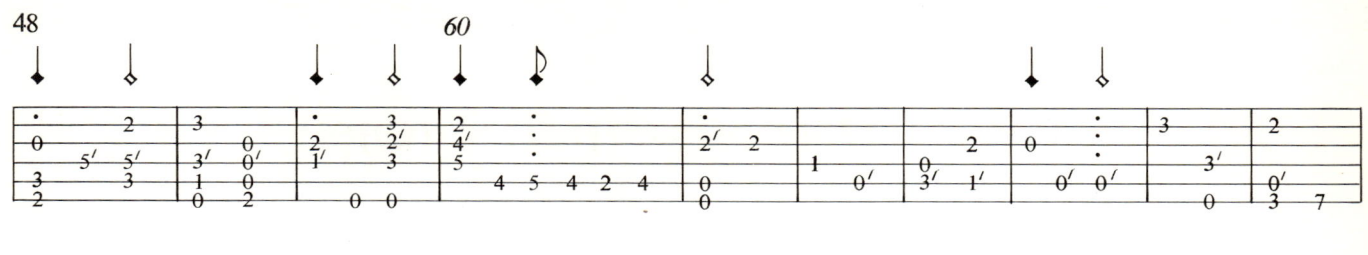

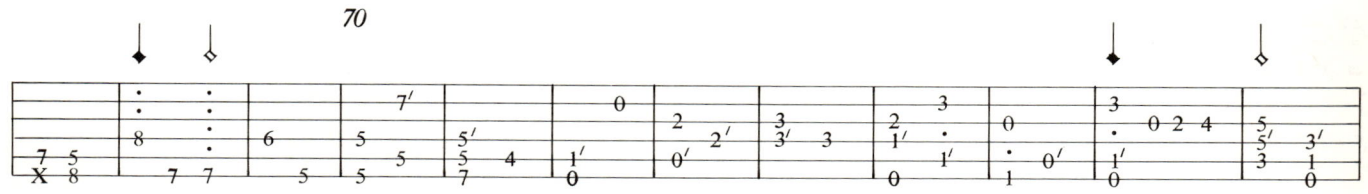

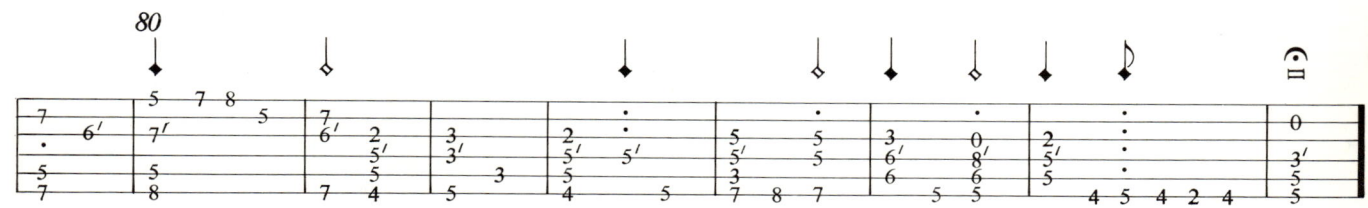

[2.] Fantasia por el segundo tono

Fantasia por el segundo tono, señalase la claue de fefaut quinta, en tercero traste.

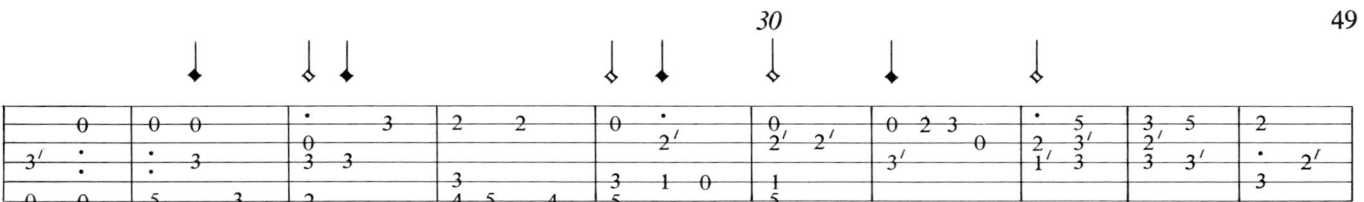
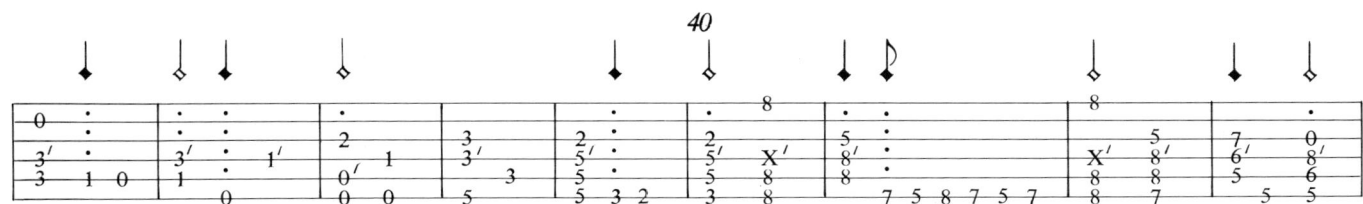
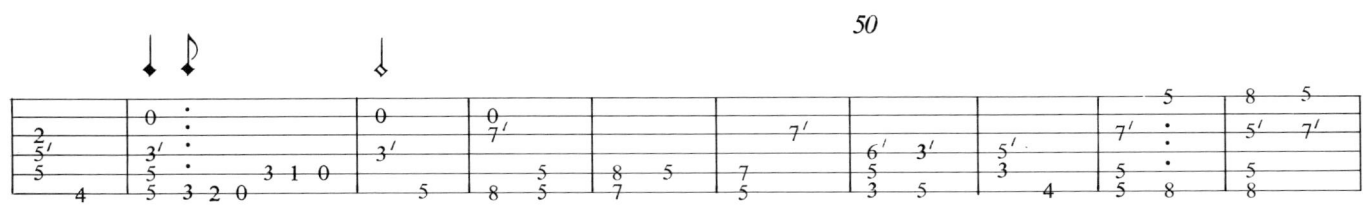
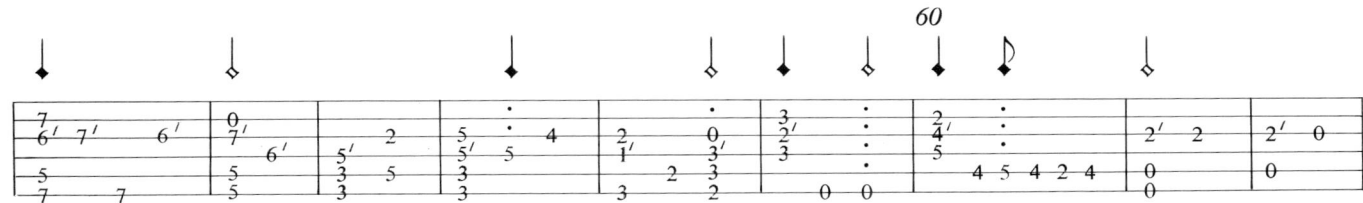
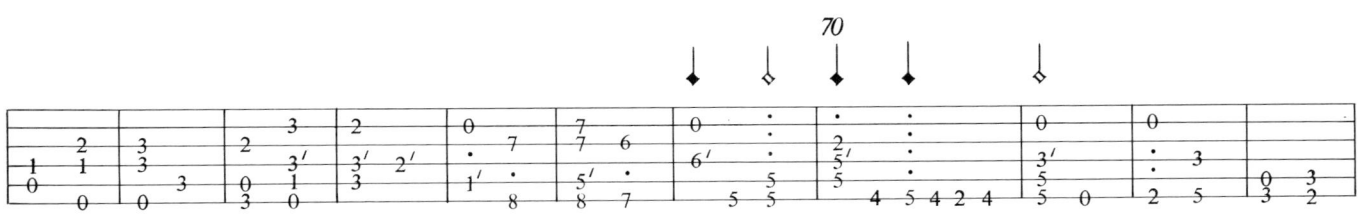
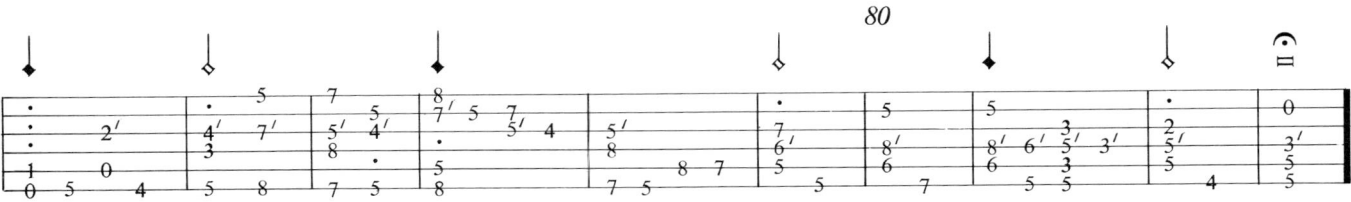

[3.] Fantasia por el tercero tono

Fantasia por el tercero tono, señalase la claue de Fefaut enla quinta en tercero traste.

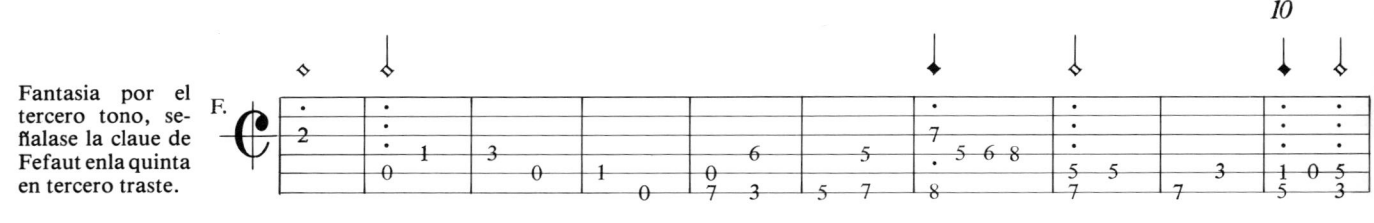

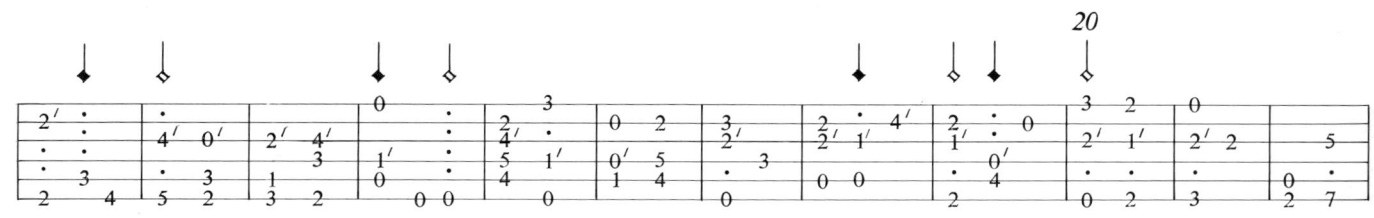

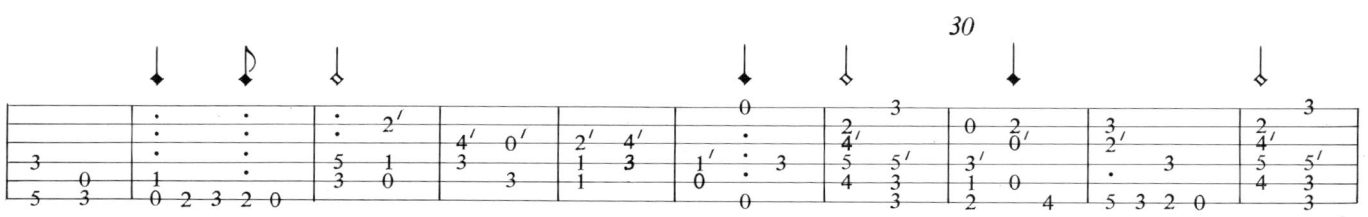

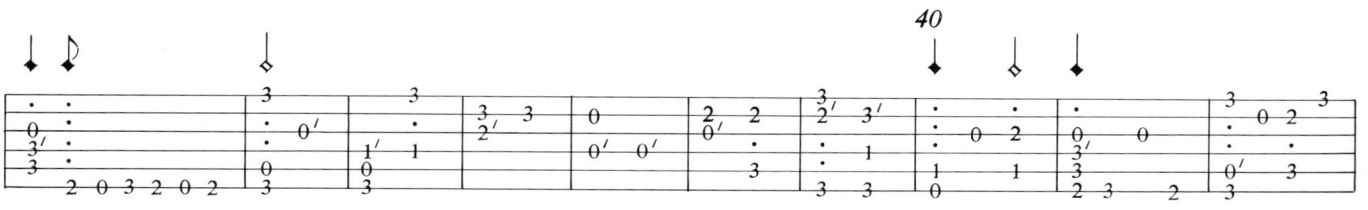

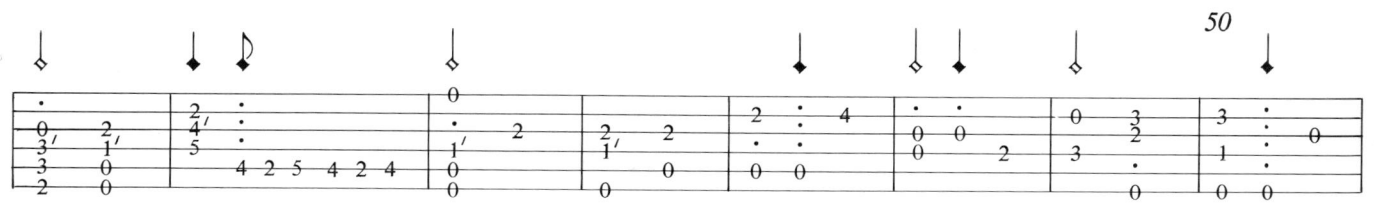

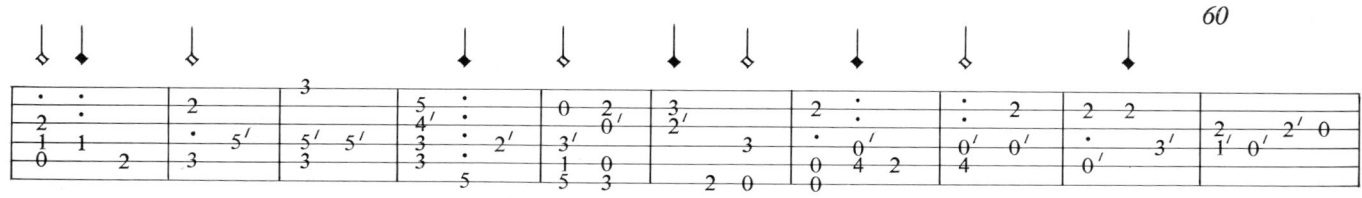

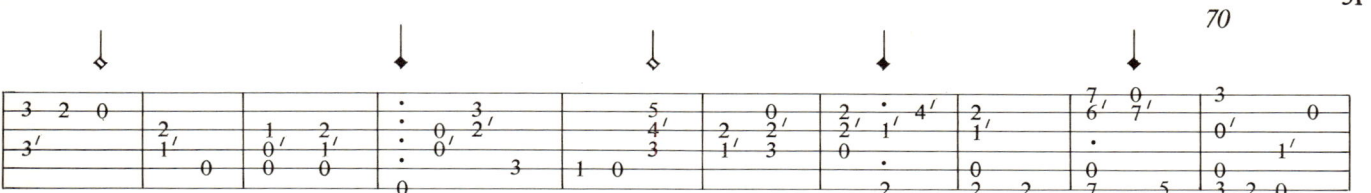
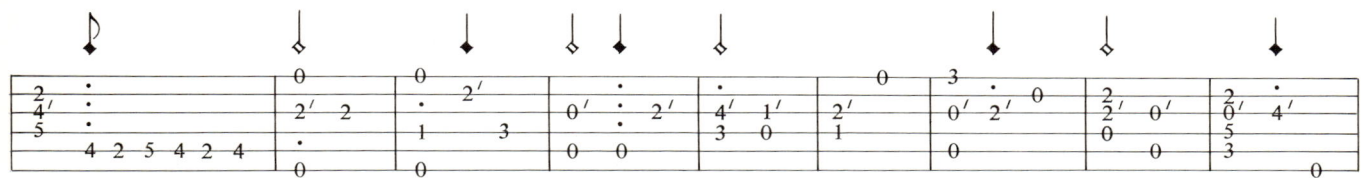
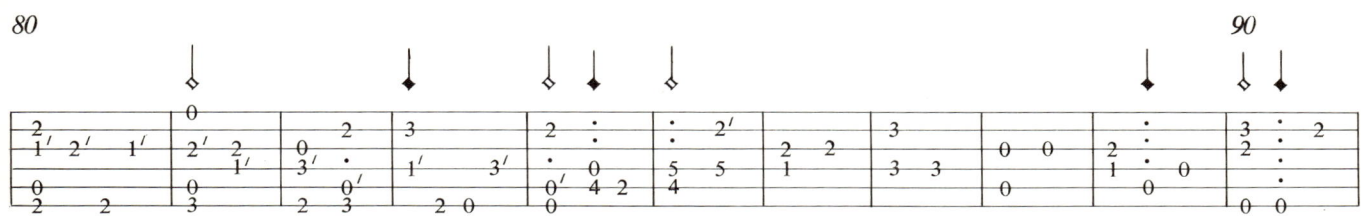
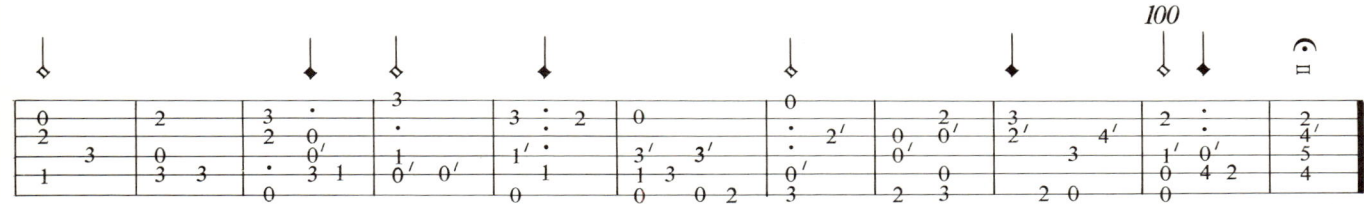

[4.] Fantasia por el quarto tono

Fãtasia por el quarto tono, señalase la claue de Fefaut q̃rta ẽ primero traste.

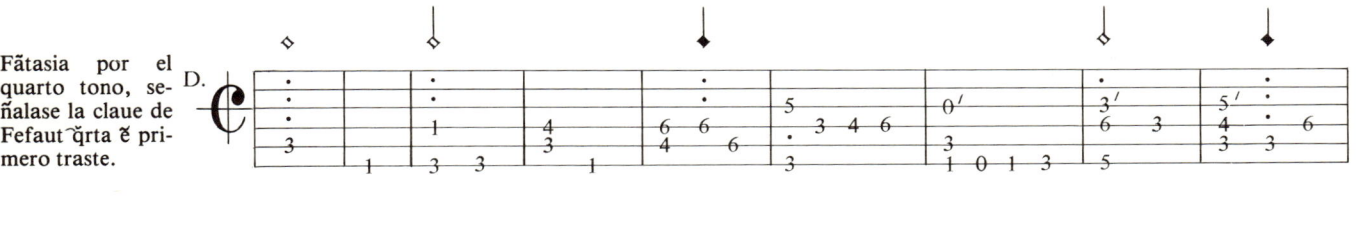
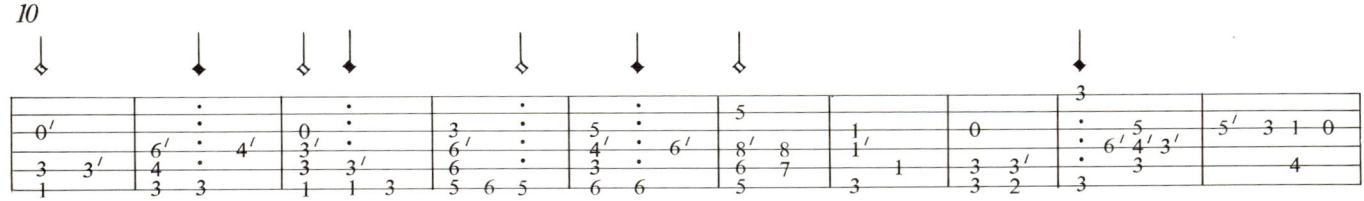

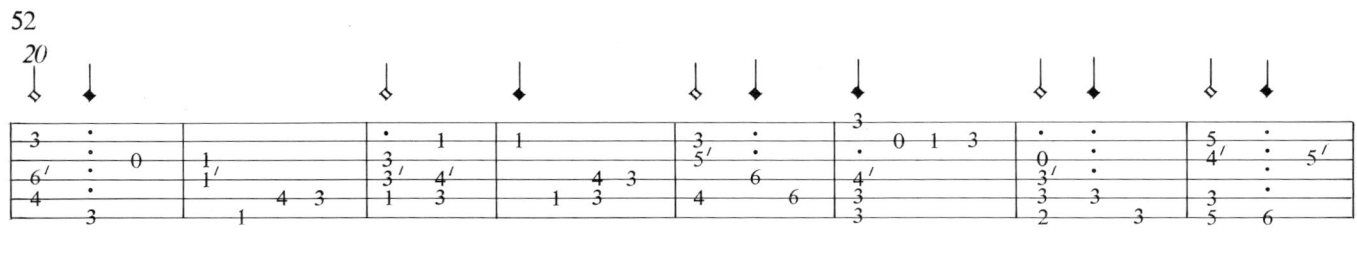
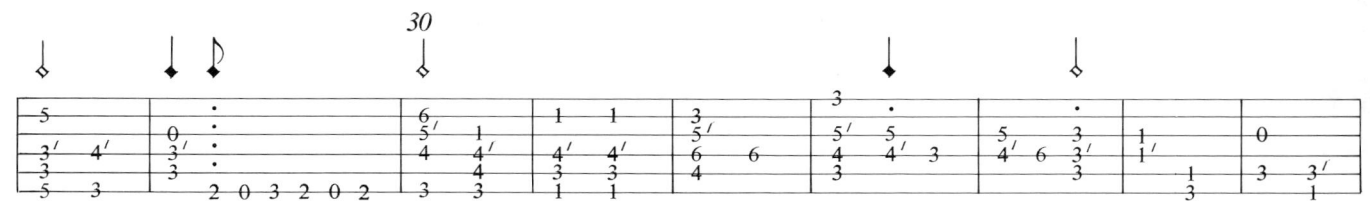
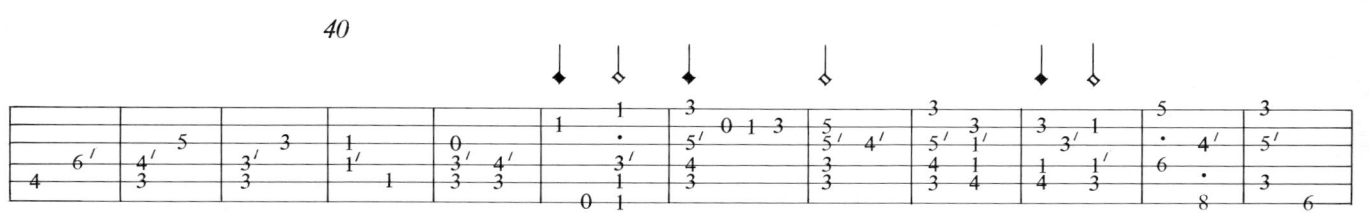
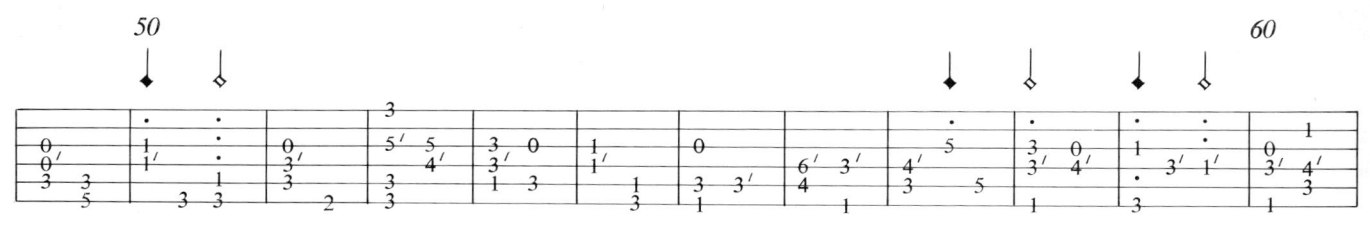
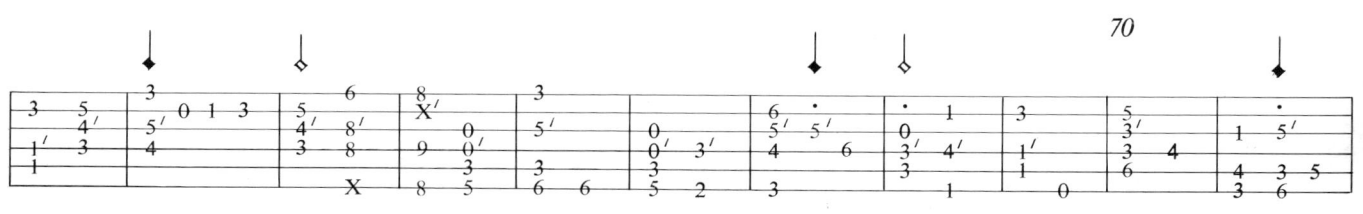
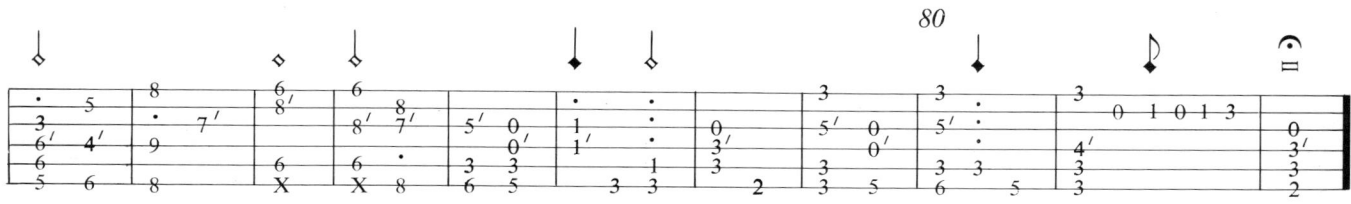

[5.] Fantasia por el quinto tono

Fantasia por el quinto tono, señalase la claue de fefaut enla quarta en vacio.

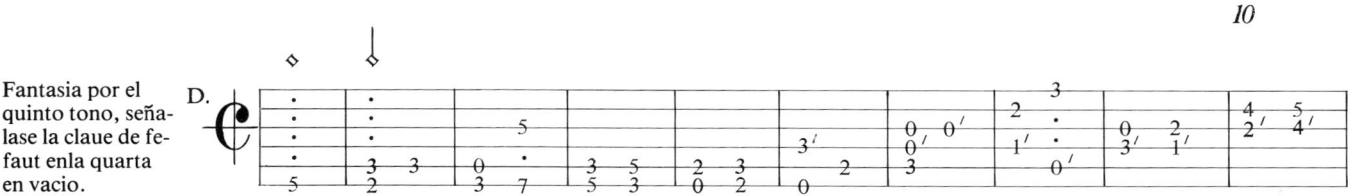

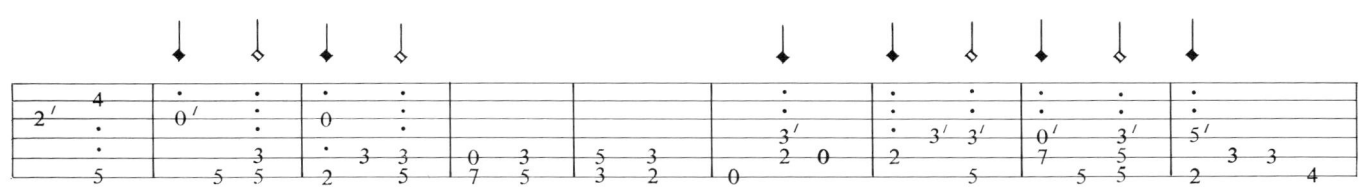

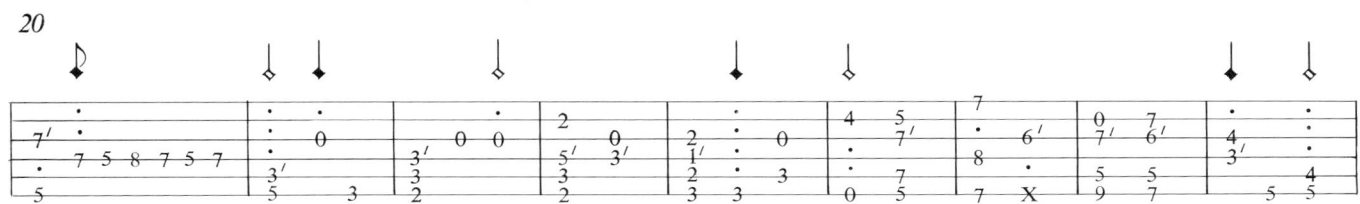

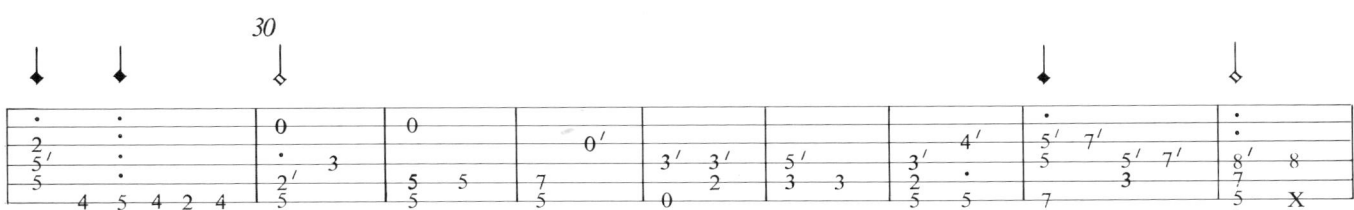

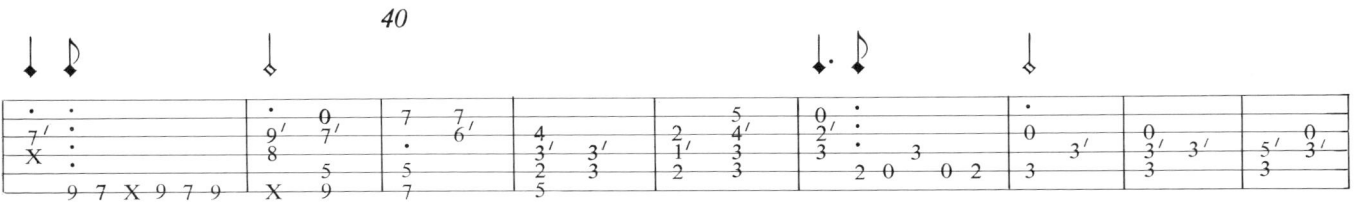

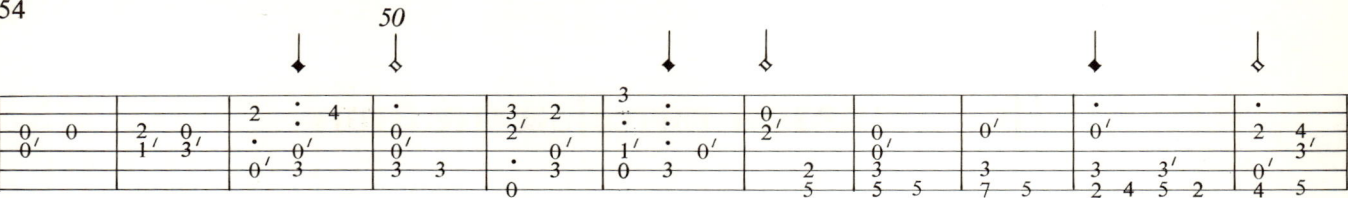
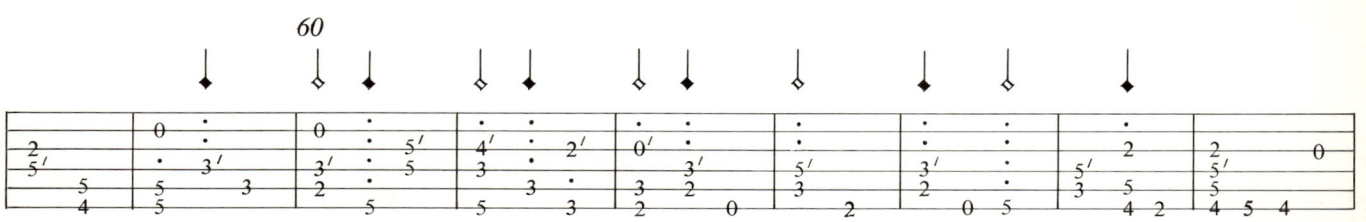
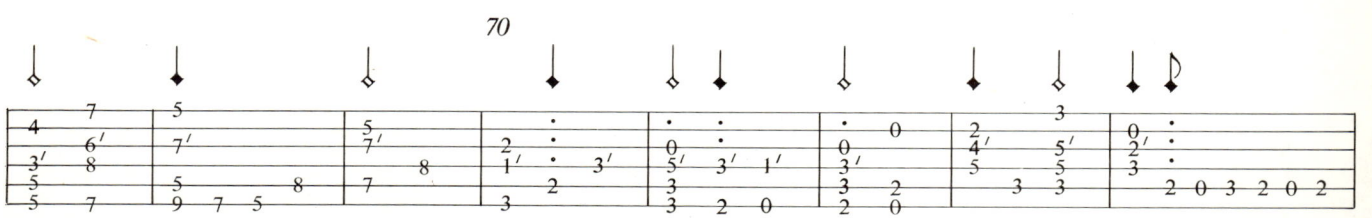
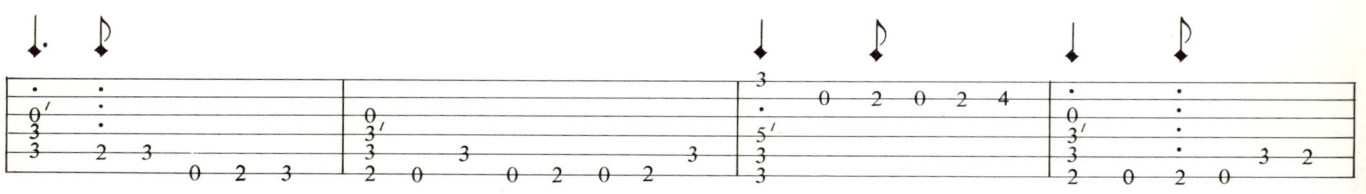
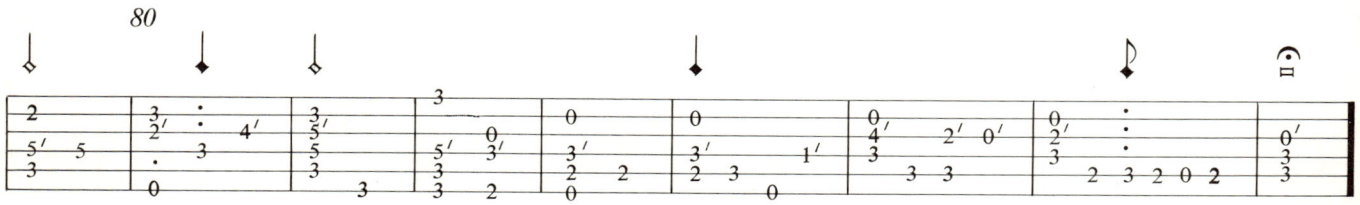

[6.] Fantasia por el sexto tono

Fãtasia por el sexto tono señalase la claue de Fefaut enla q̃rta en segũdo traste.

[7.] Fantasia por el septimo tono

Fantasia por el septimo tono señalase la claue de Fefaut en la quinta en tercero traste.

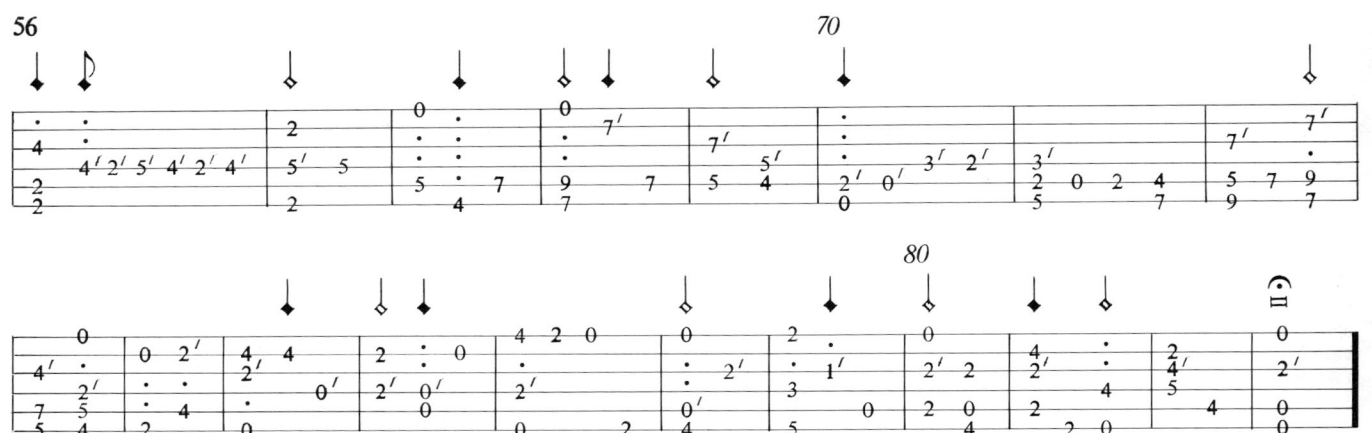

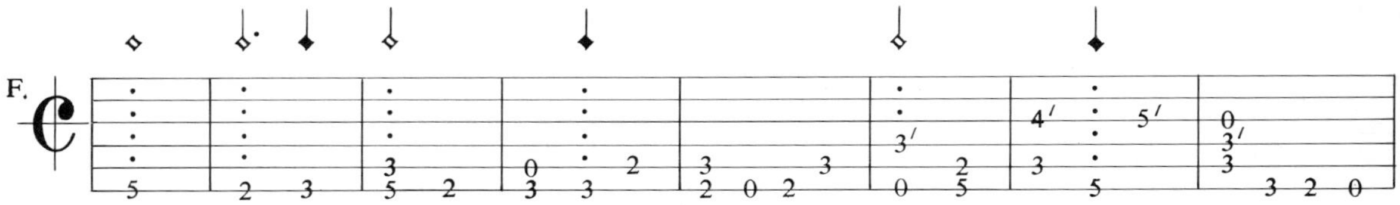

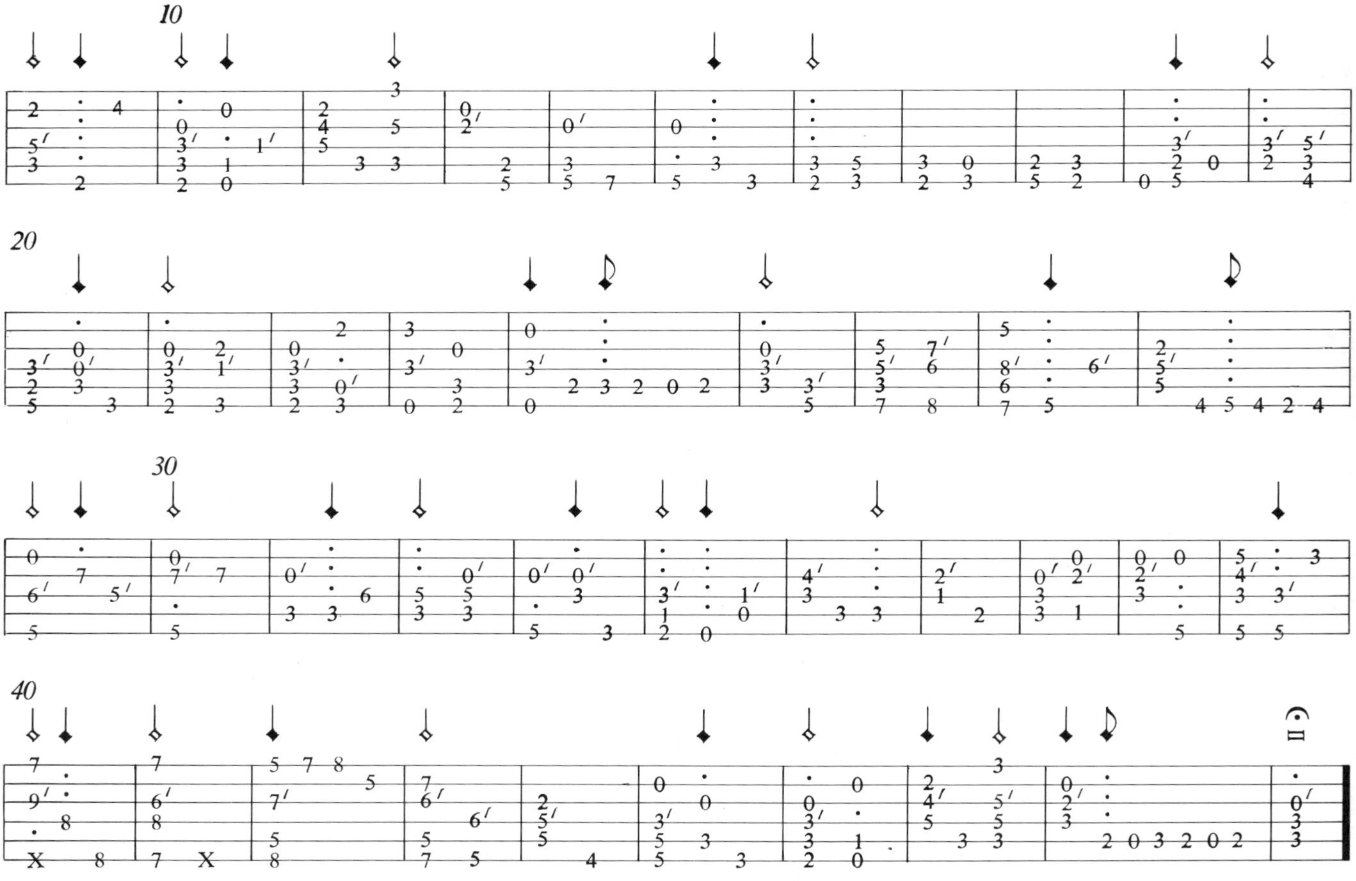

[8.] Fantasia por el octauo tono

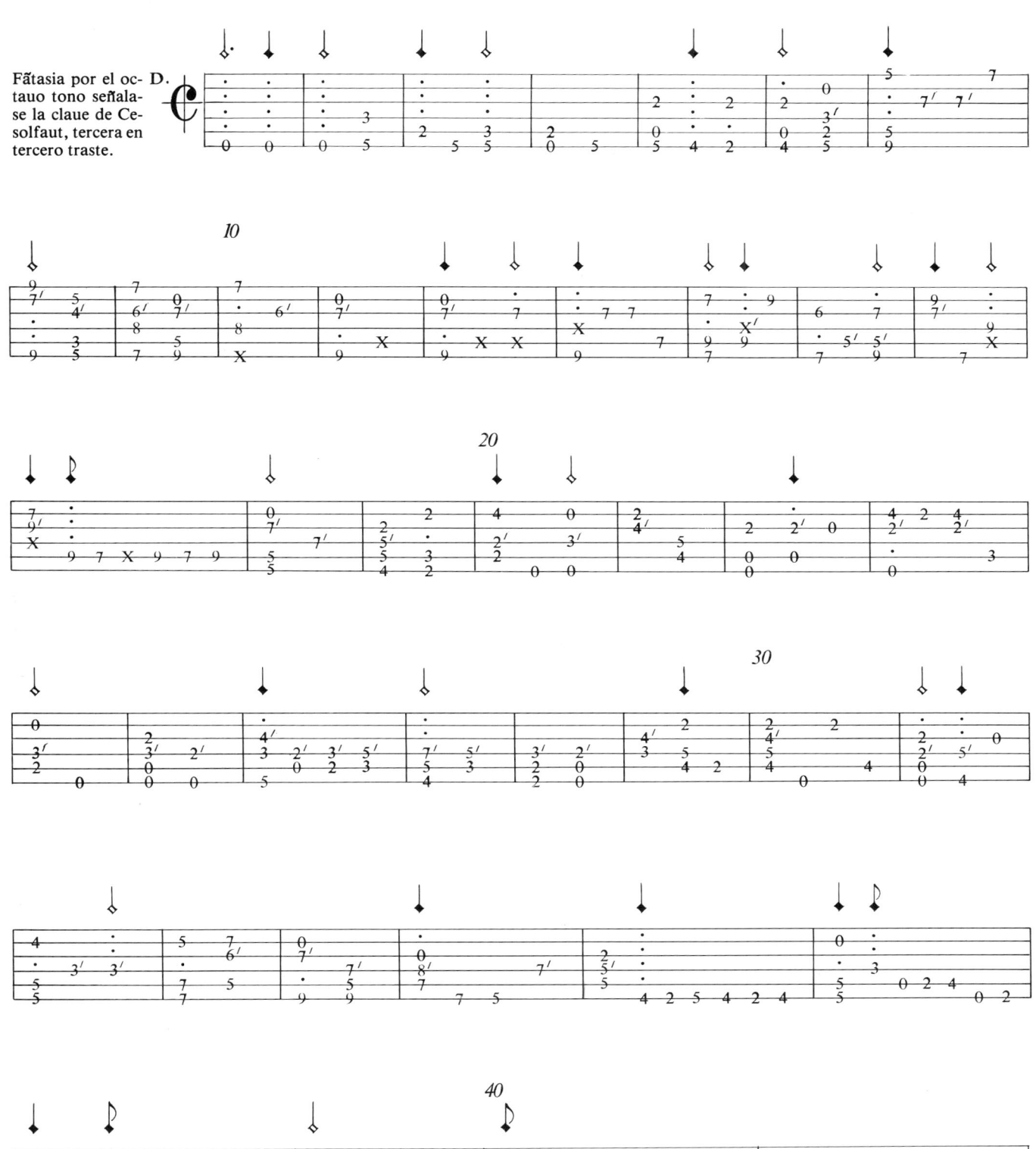

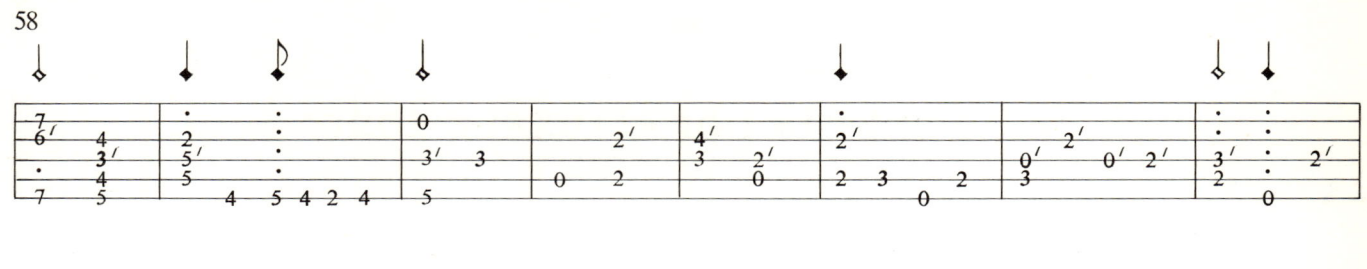

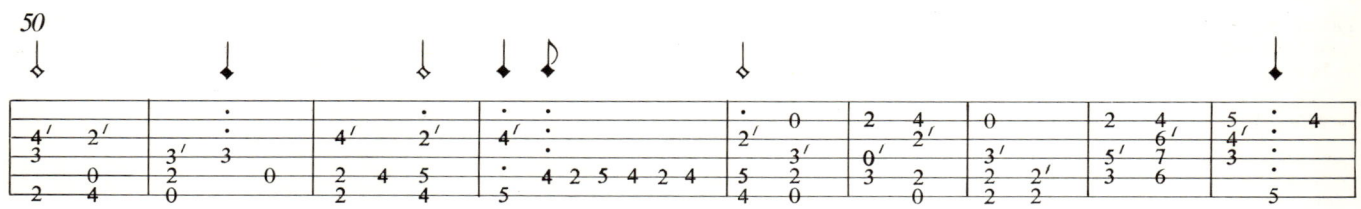

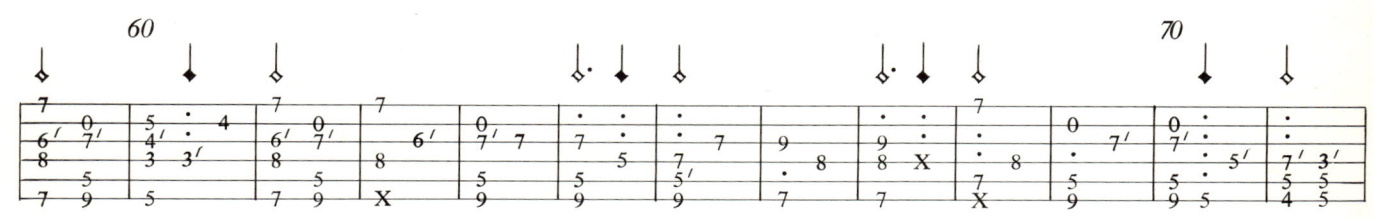

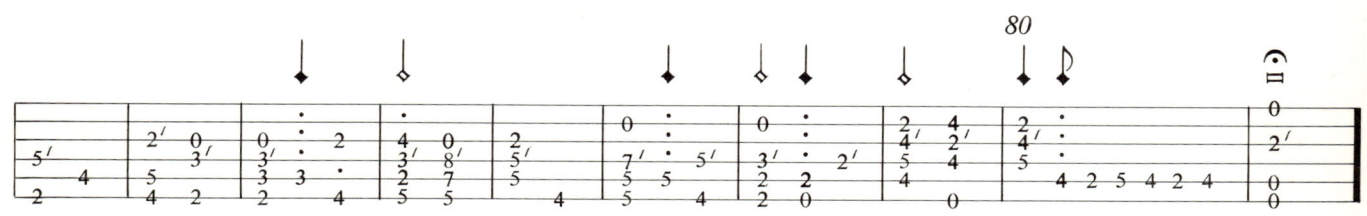

[9.] Fantasia a tres, por el primer tono

Siguēse ciertas Fā-
tasias a tres, y se-
ñalase la voz de en
medio con vnos
puntillos que es el
alto y esta primera
es del primer tono,
señalase la claue
de fefaut tercera
en primer Traste.

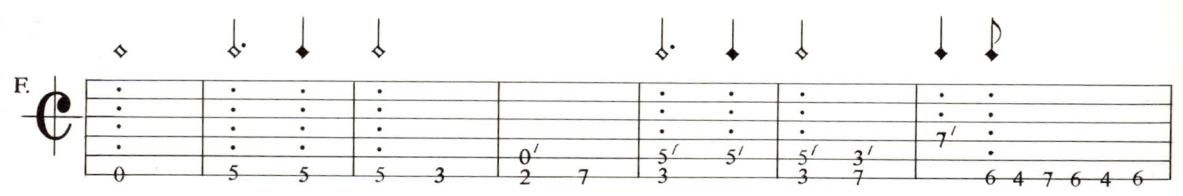

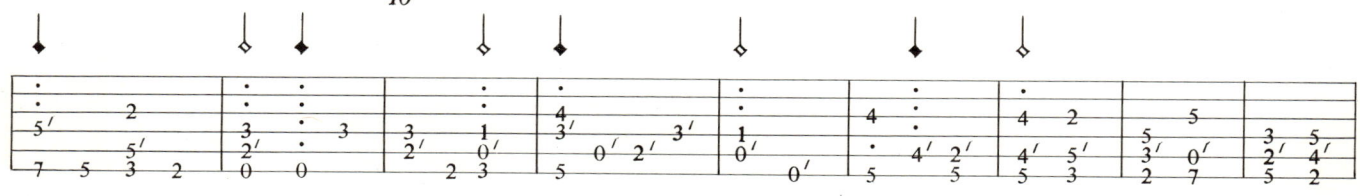

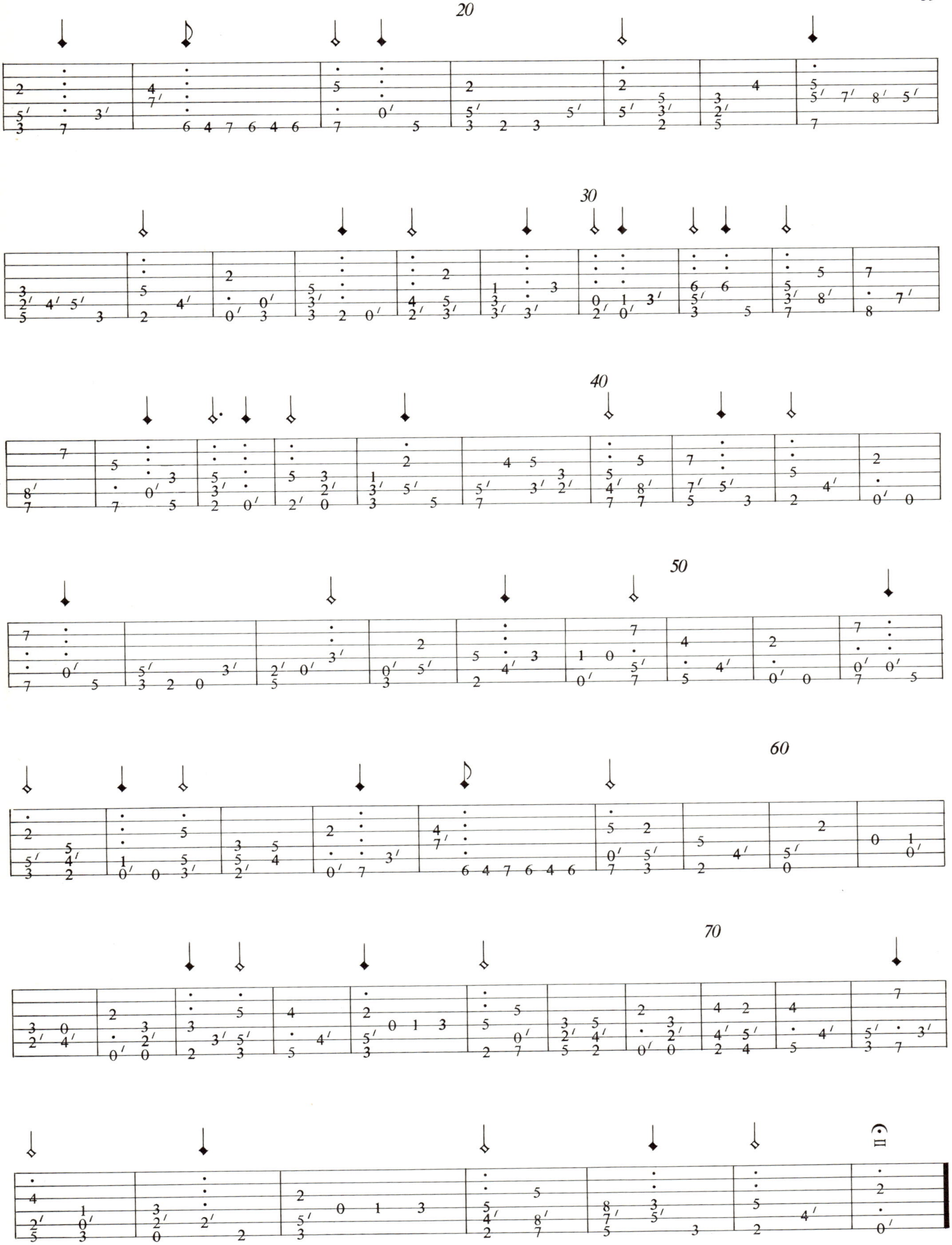

[10.] Fantasia a tres, por el quinto tono

Fantasia por el quinto tono a tres, señalase la claue de Fefaut, enla quarta en vacio.

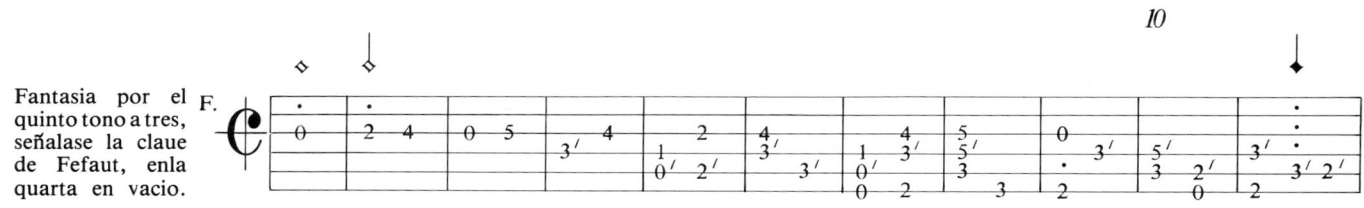
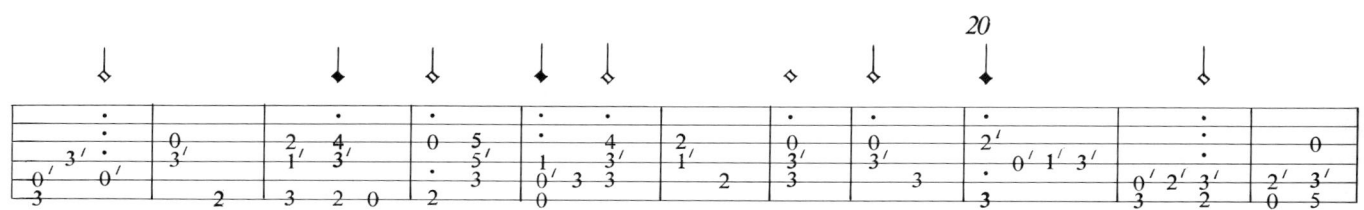
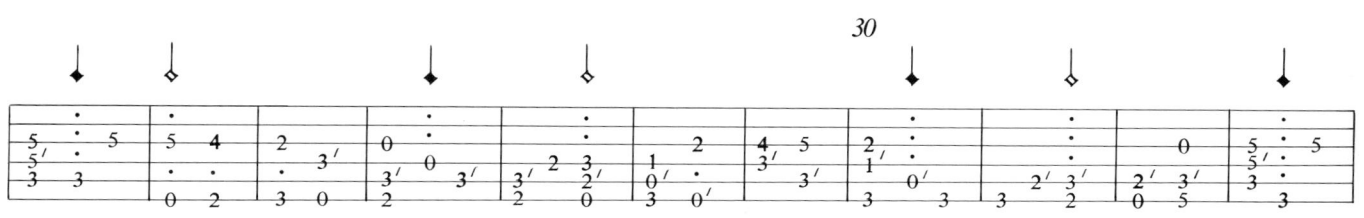
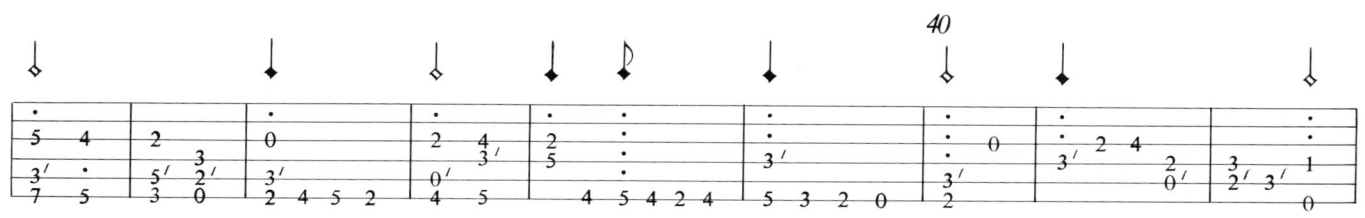
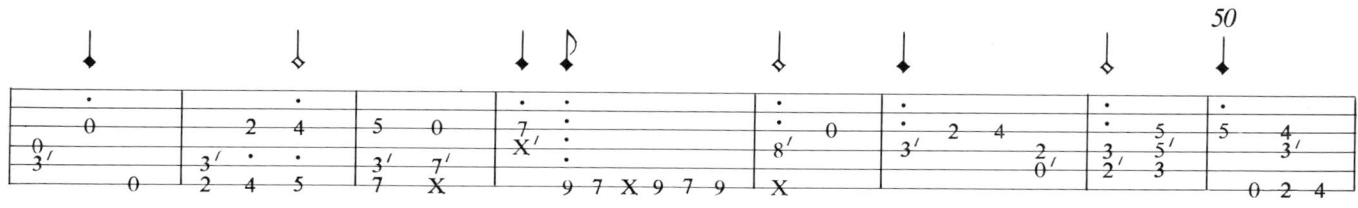

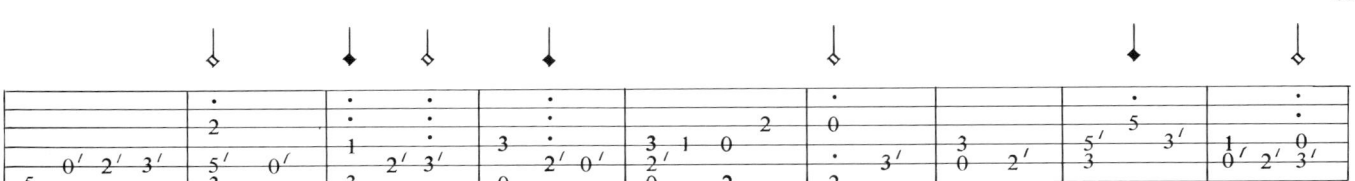

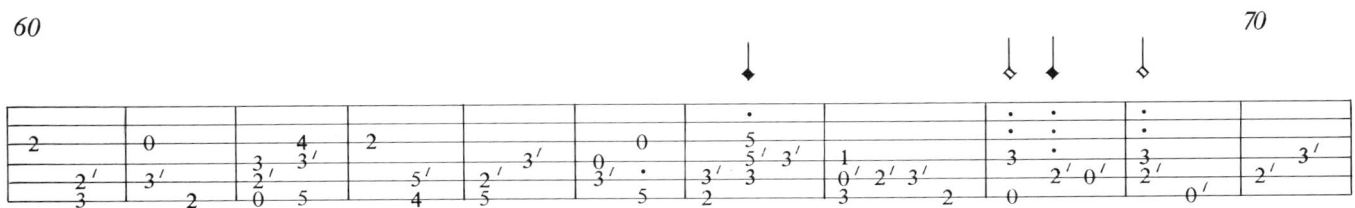

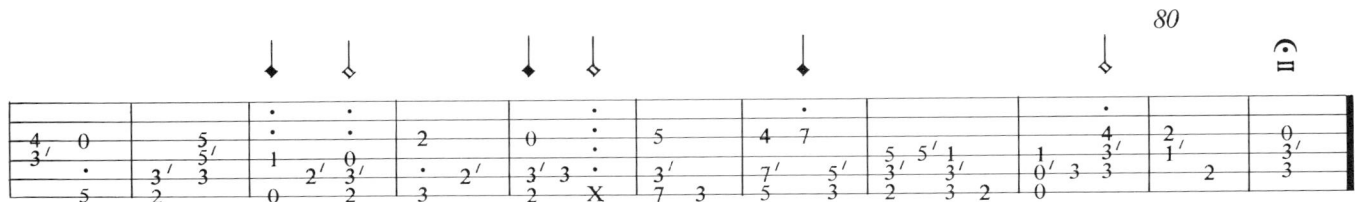

[11.] Fantasia a tres, por el septimo tono

Fantasia por el septimo tono a tres, señalase la claue de Fefaut quinta en tercero traste.

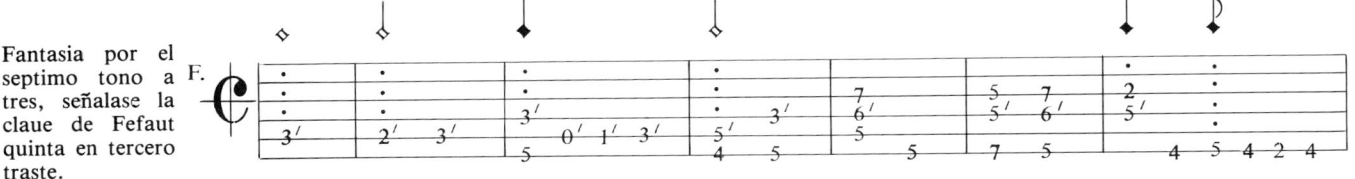

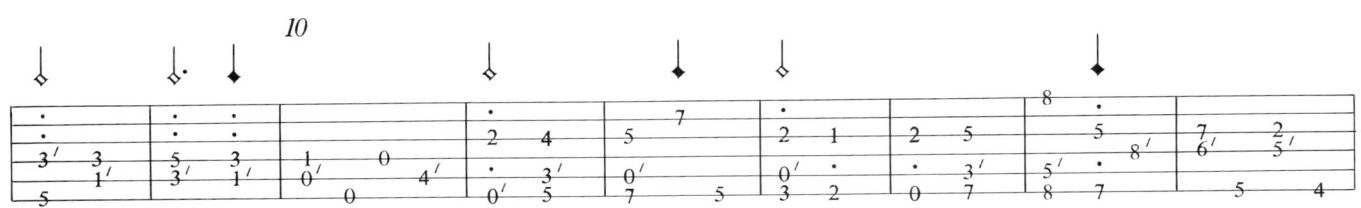

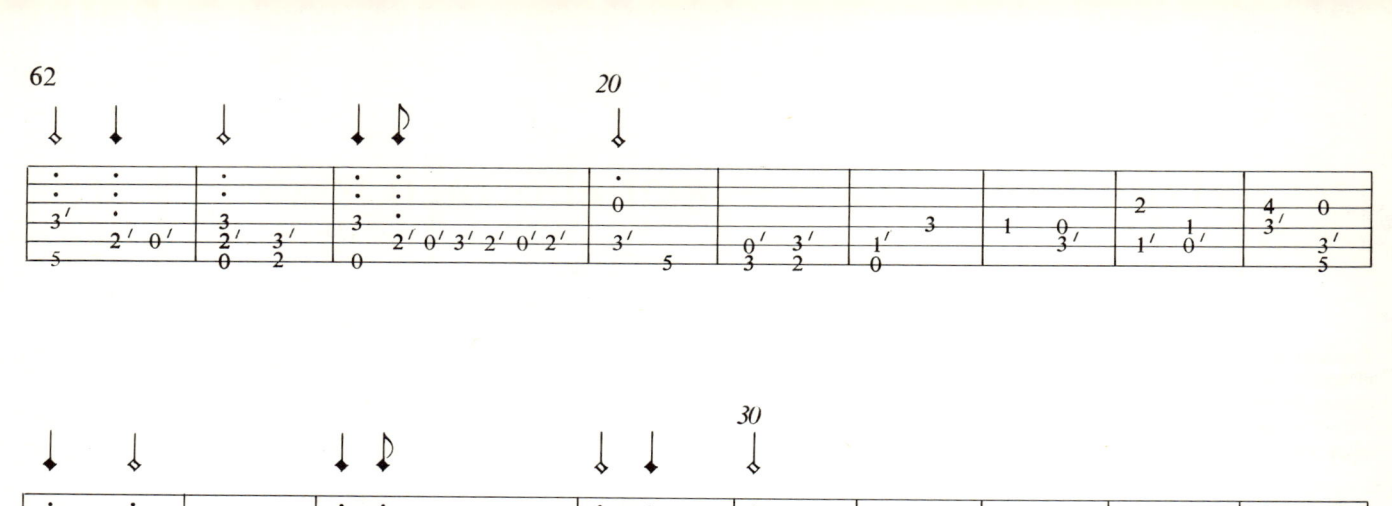
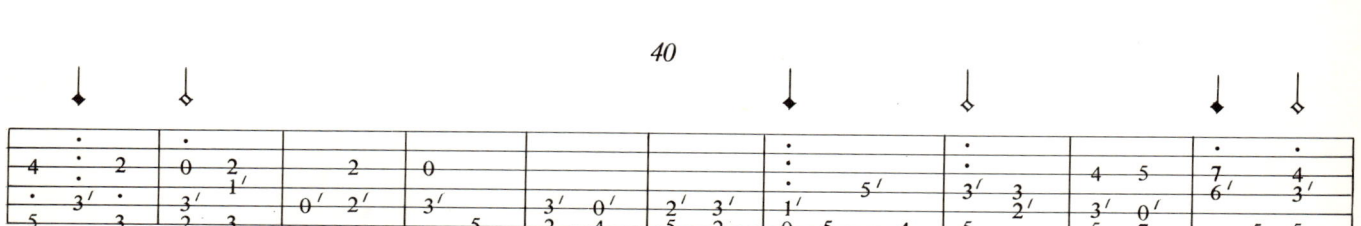
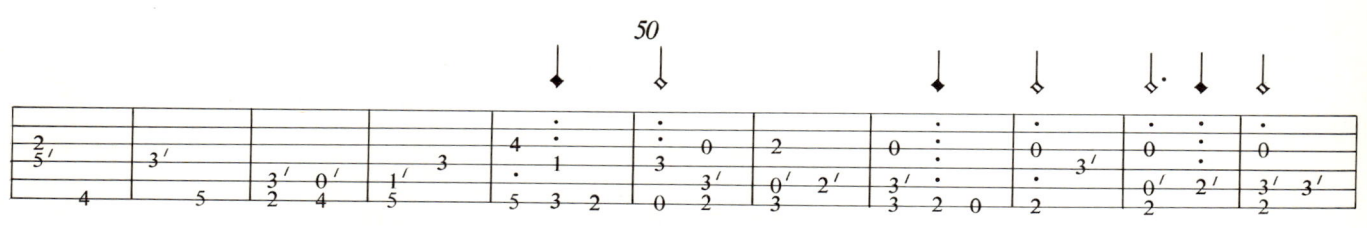
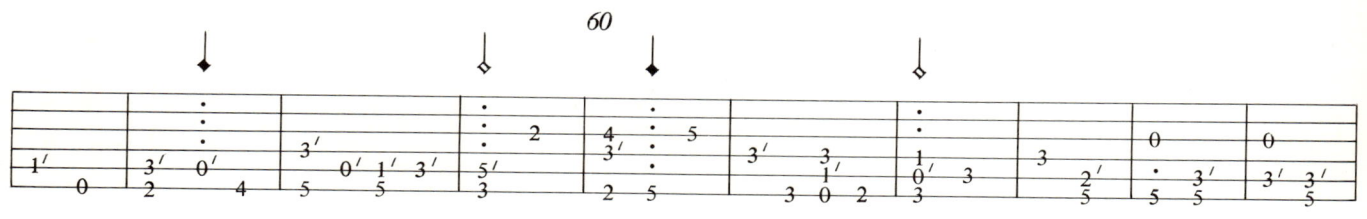
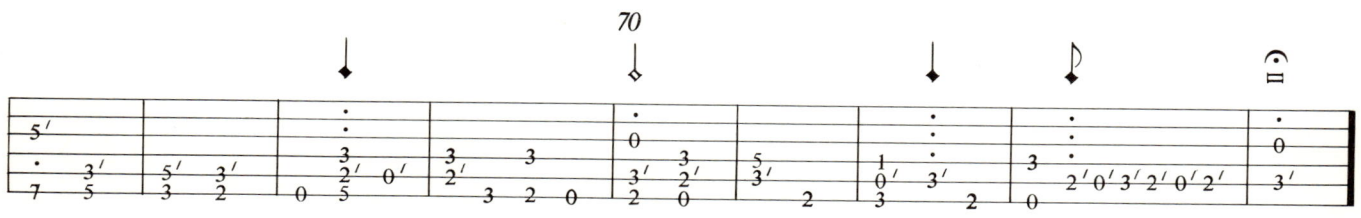

[12.] Fantasia a tres, por el octauo tono

Fantasia a 3. por el octauo tono, señalase la claue de Fefaut en la quarta en vacio.

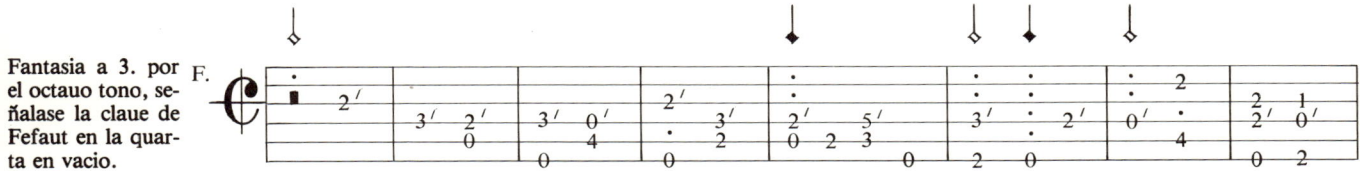
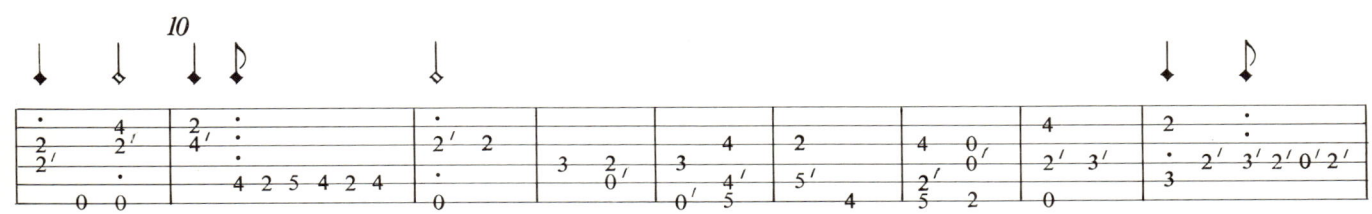
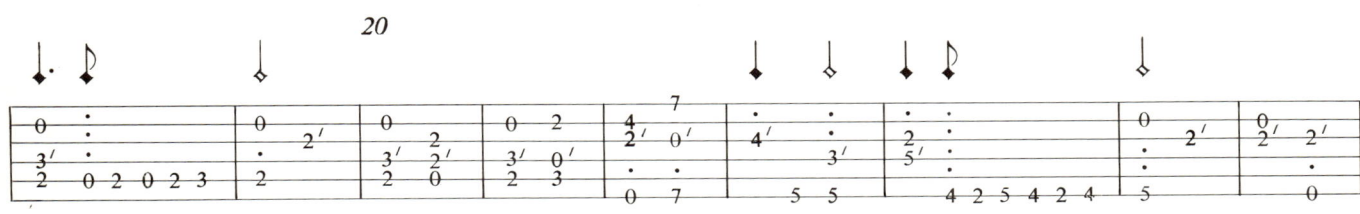
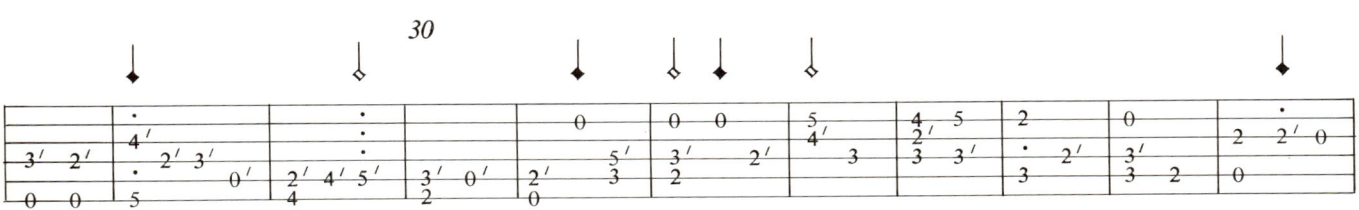
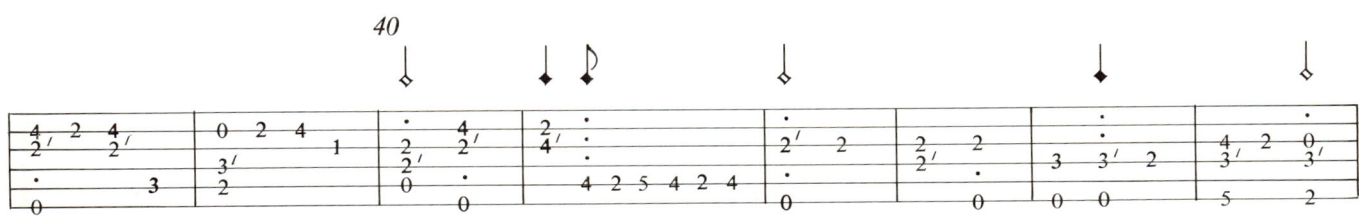

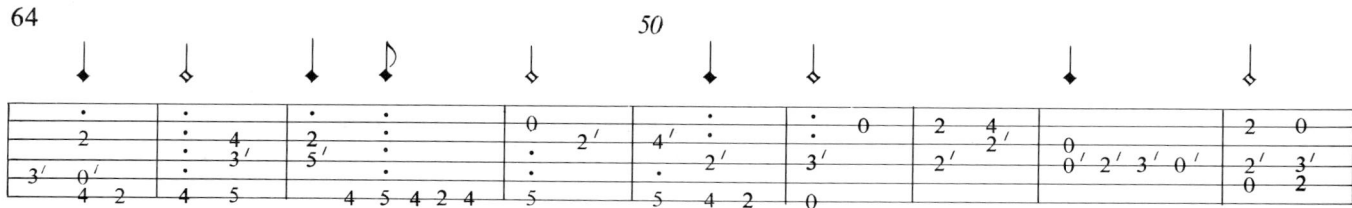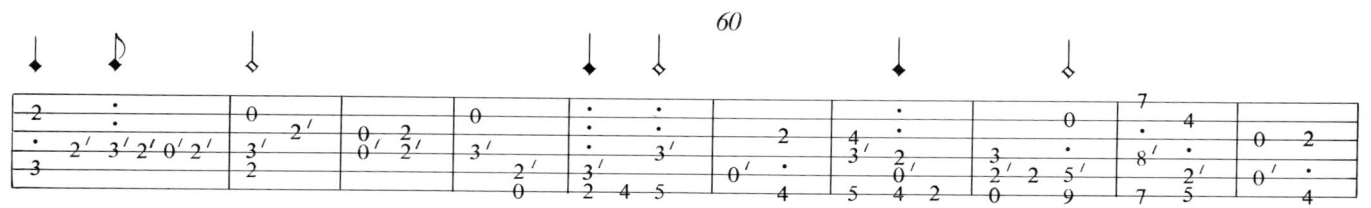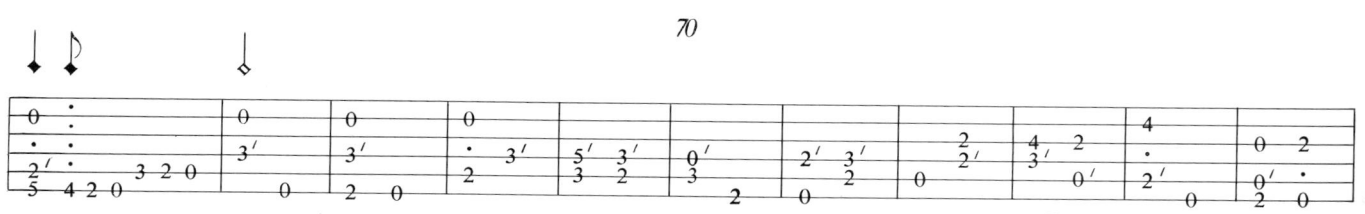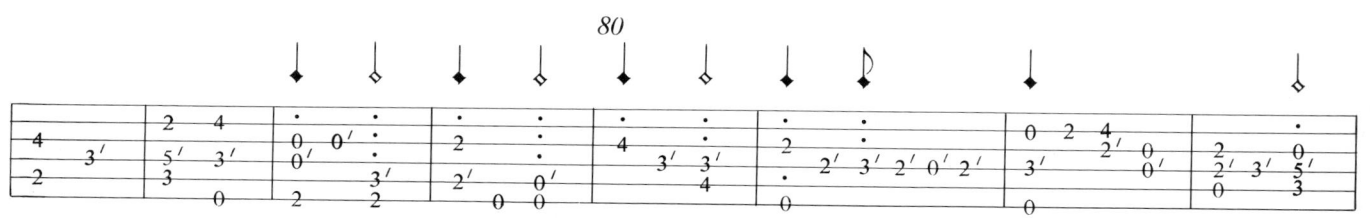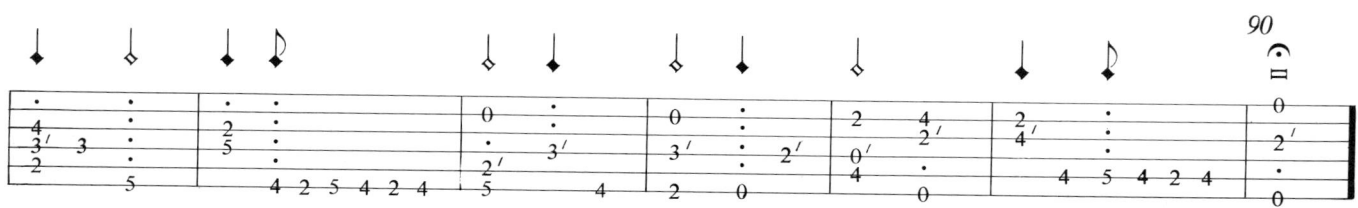

[13.] Fantasia por el primer tono

Fantasia por el primero tono a quatro, señalase la claue de Fefaut quarta en vacio, y señalase la voz del Tenor con vnos puntillos, y en todas las demas que se siguen.

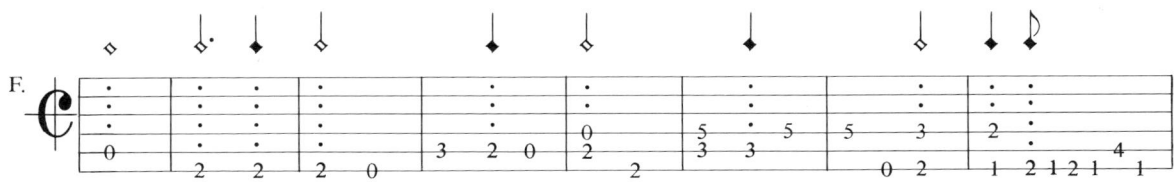
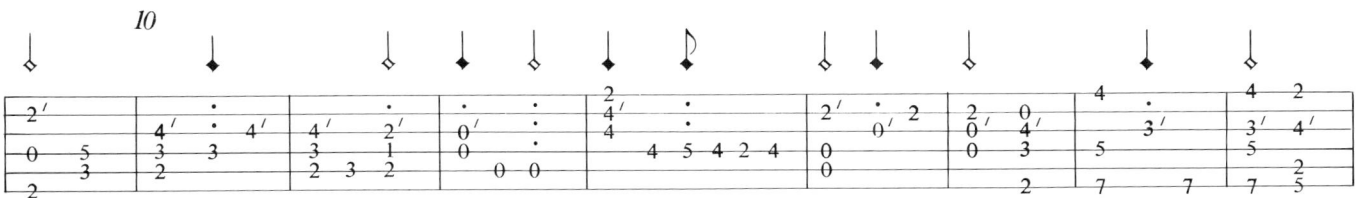
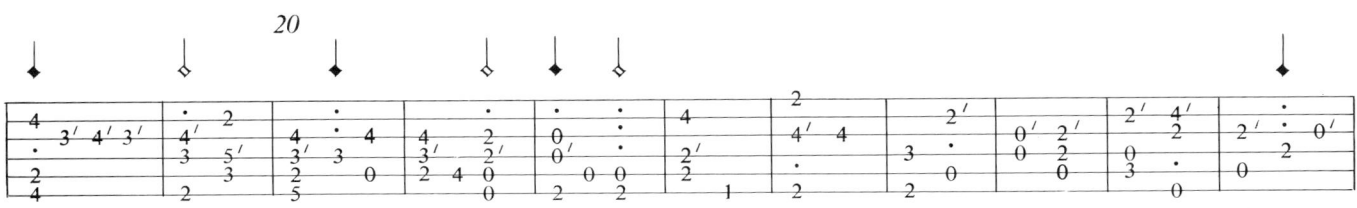
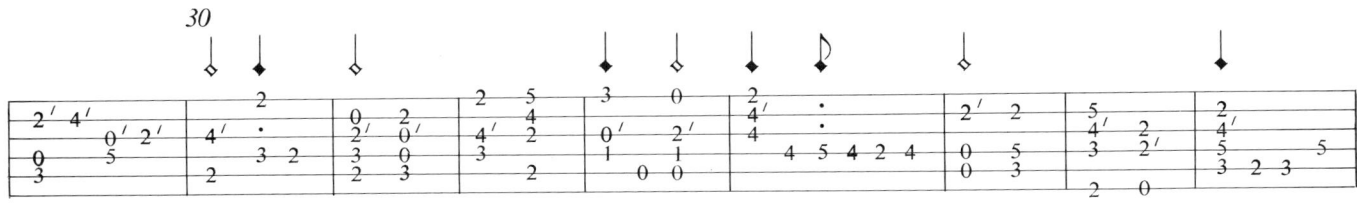
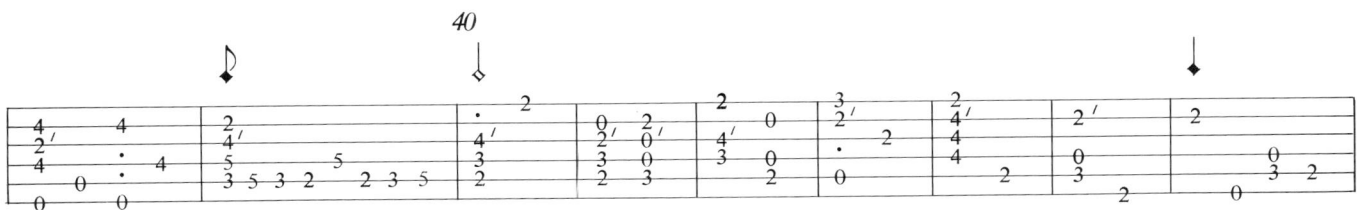

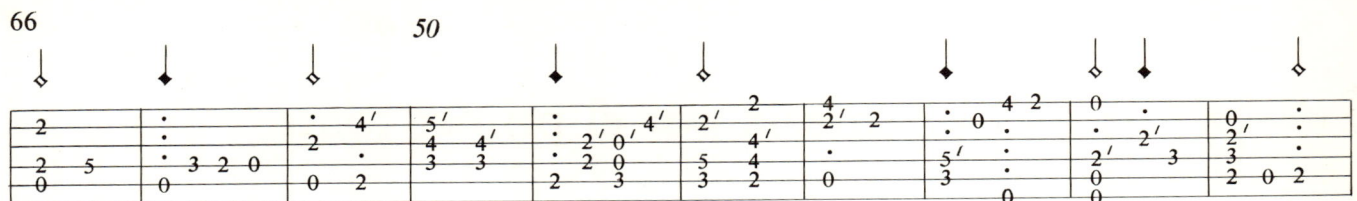

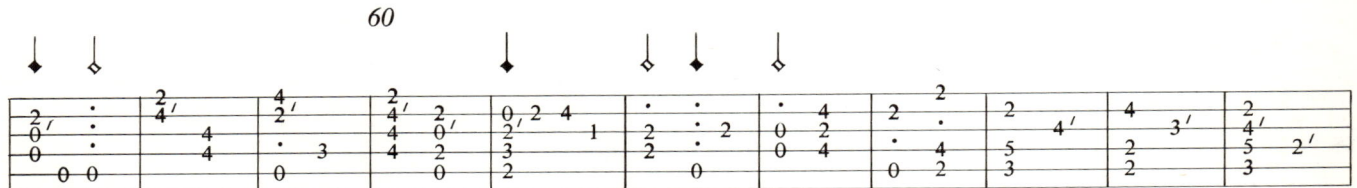

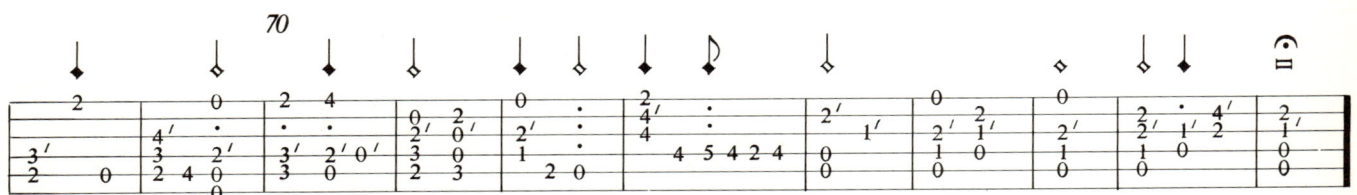

[14.] Fanta[sia] por el pri[mer] tono, por gesolreut

Fantasia por el primero tono, por Gsolreut a quatro, señalasse la claue de Fefaut tercera en tercero traste.

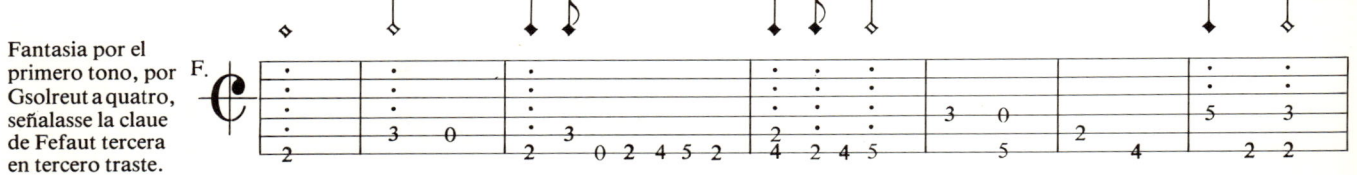

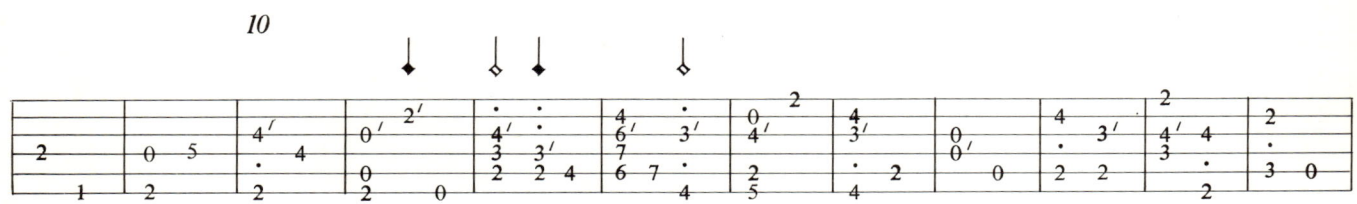

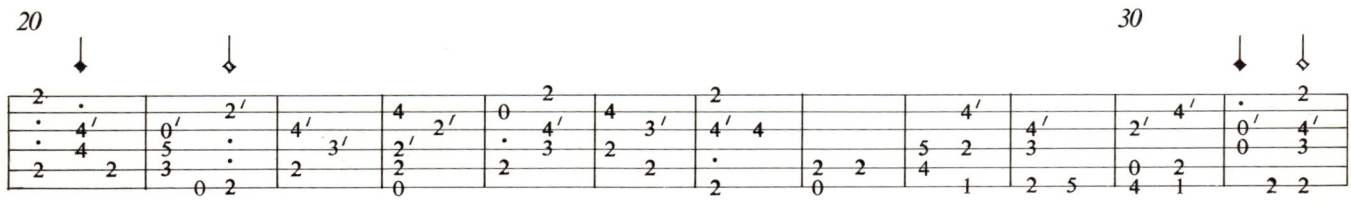

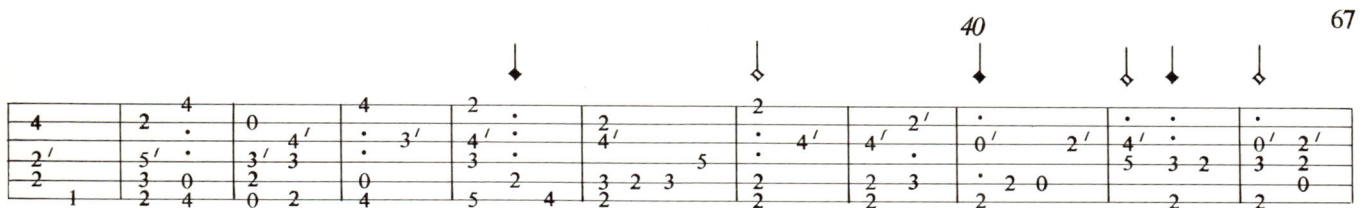
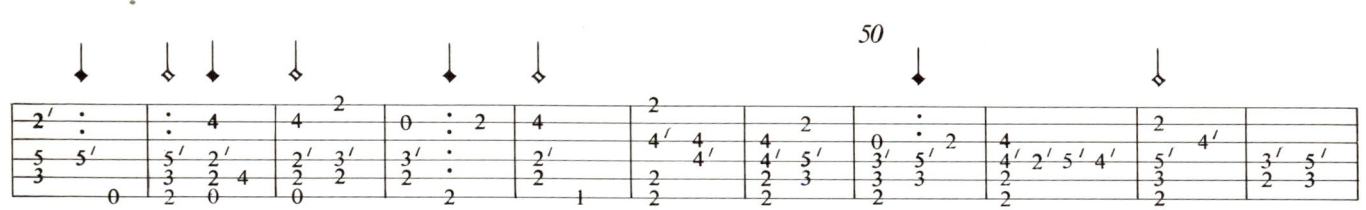
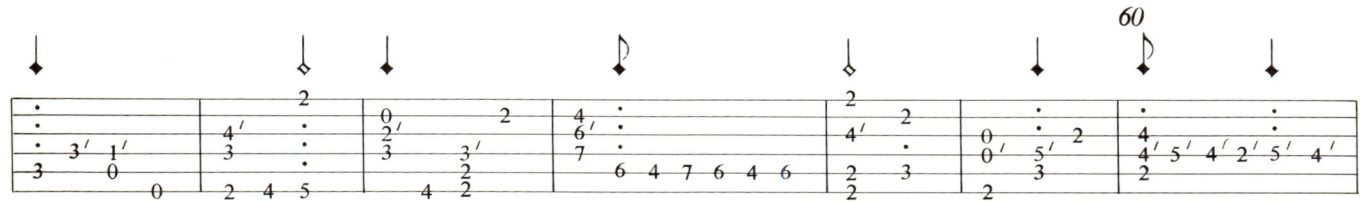
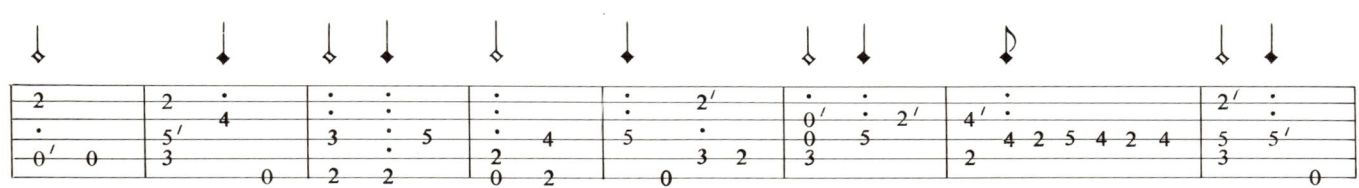
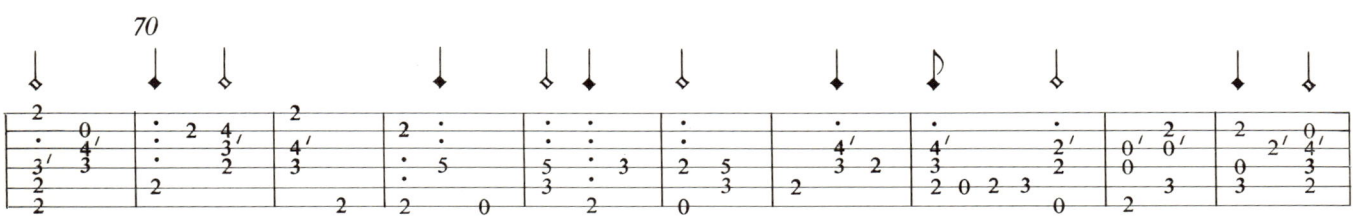
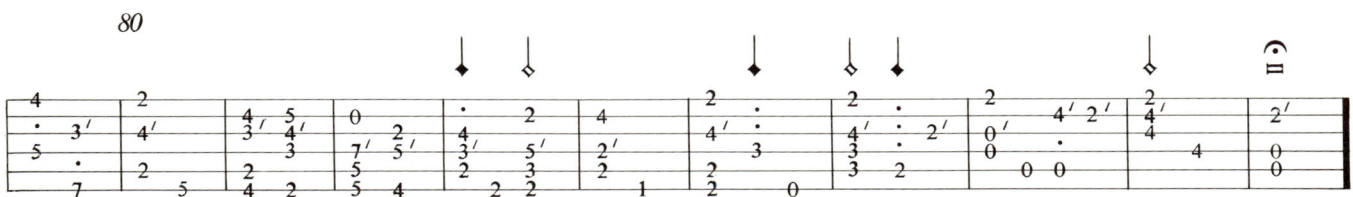

[15.] Fa[n]ta[sia] por el segu[ndo] tono, por gesolreut

Fantasia por el segundo tono a quatro por Gsolreut, señalase la claue de Fefaut en la quarta en vacio, y lleua alguna glossa.

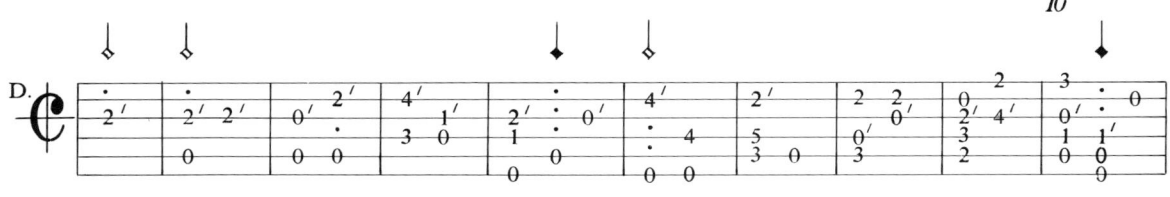
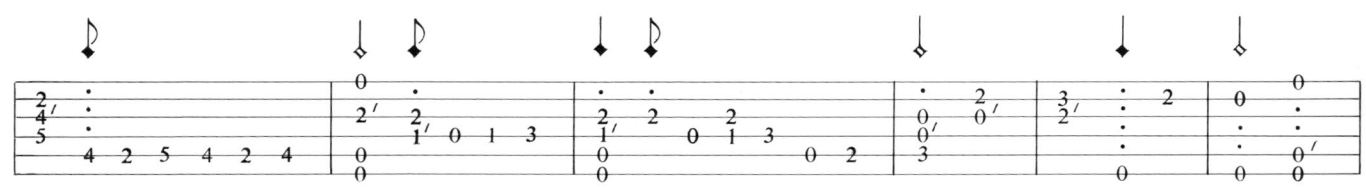
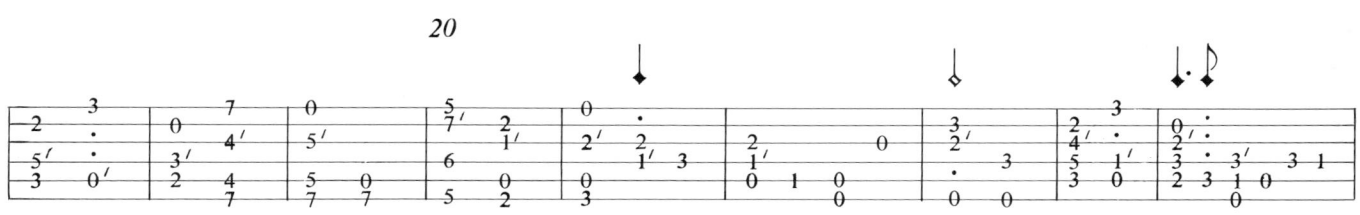
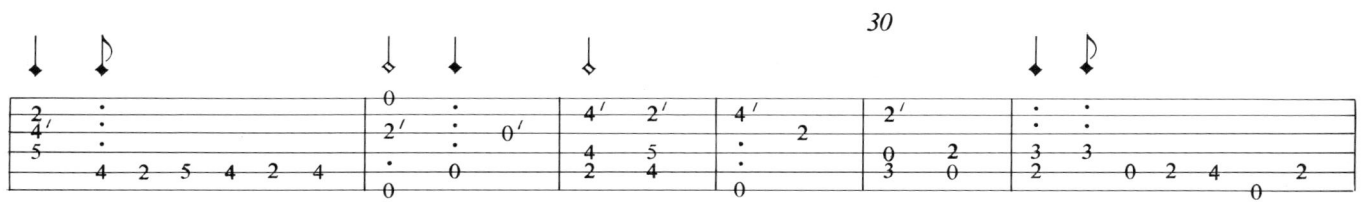
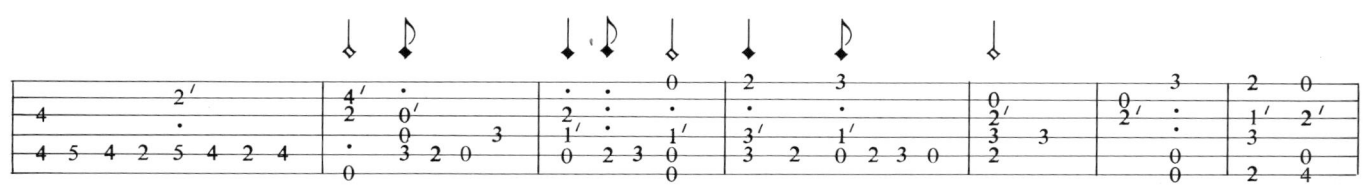
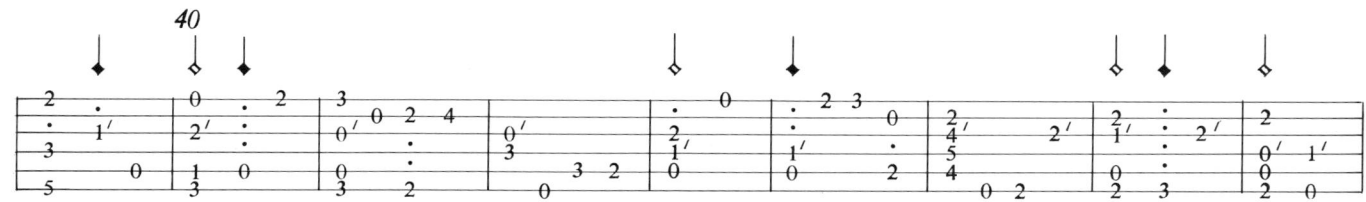

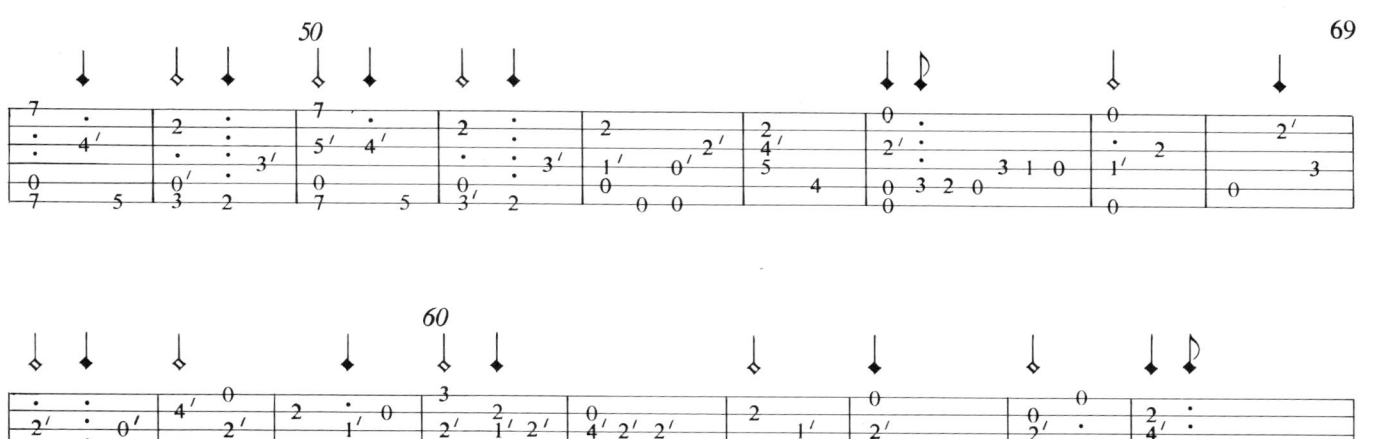

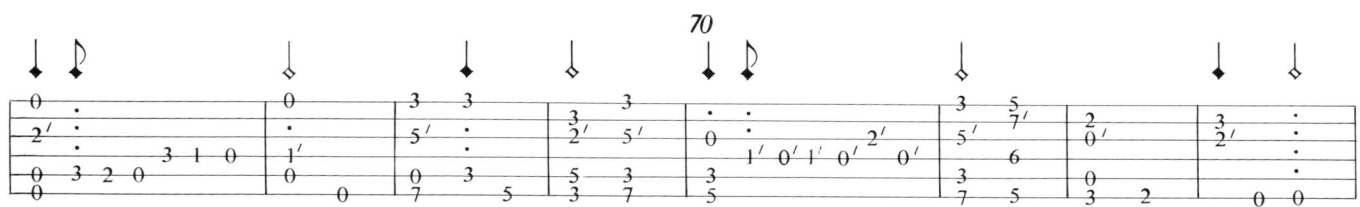

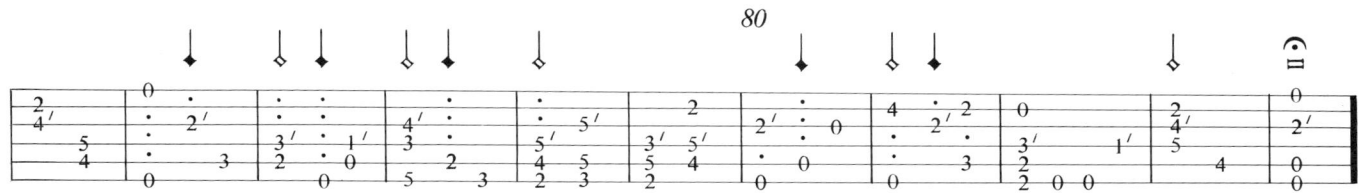

[16.] Fanta[sia] por [el] quarto tono, por alamire

Fantasia a quatro por el quarto tono por alamire, señalase la claue de Fefaut quarta en vacio.

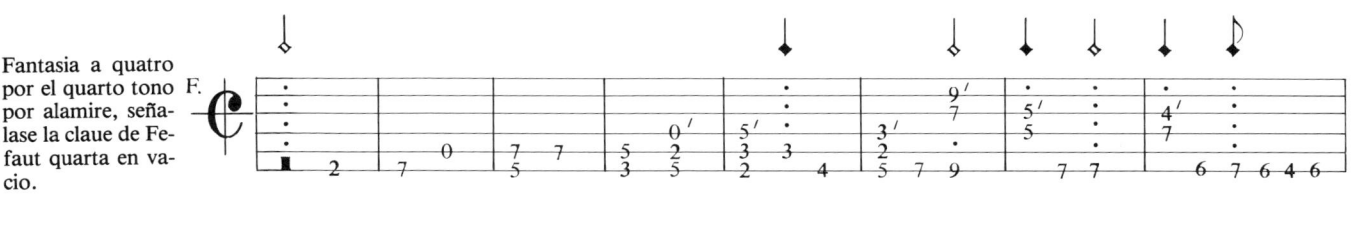

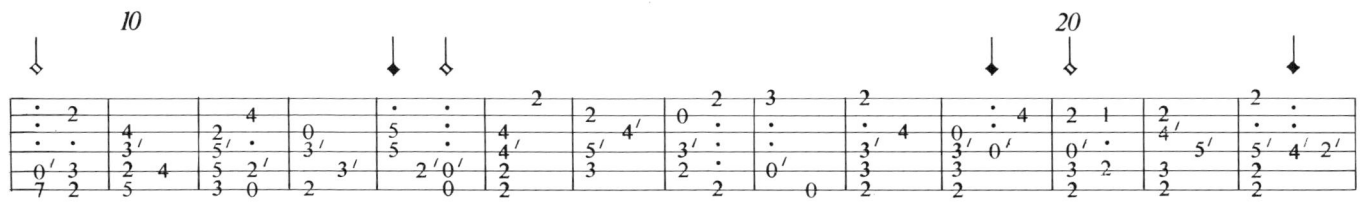

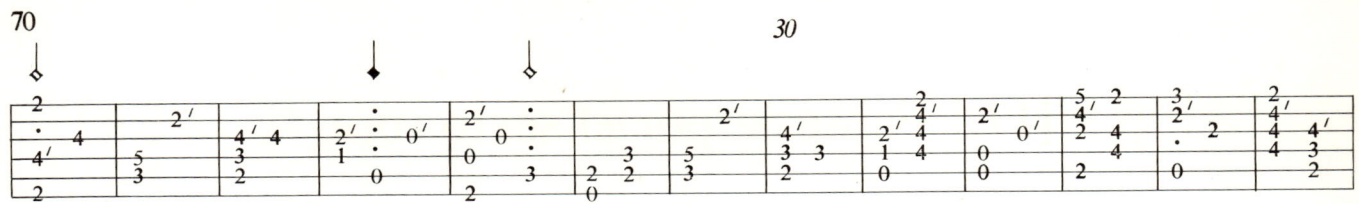
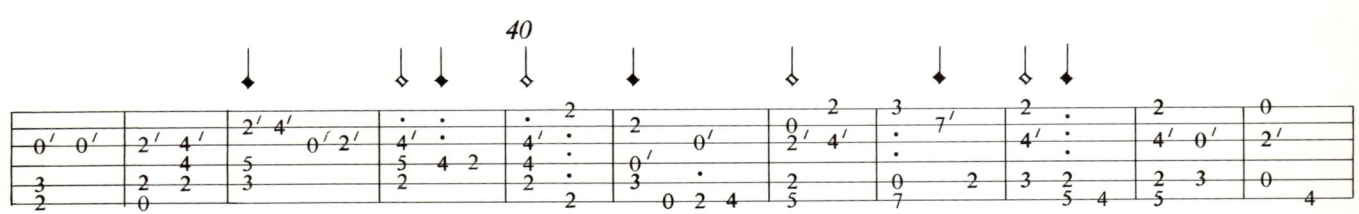
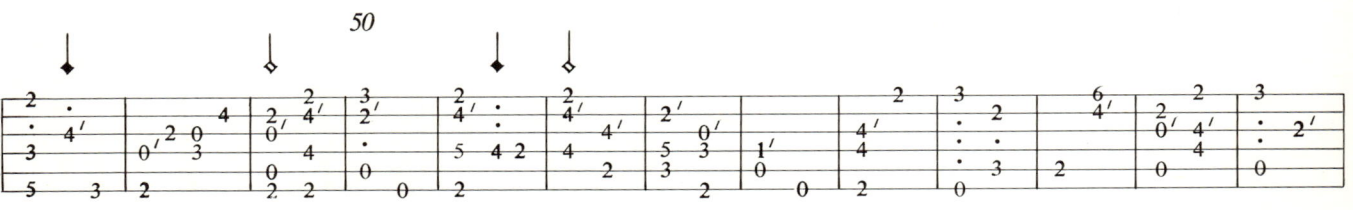
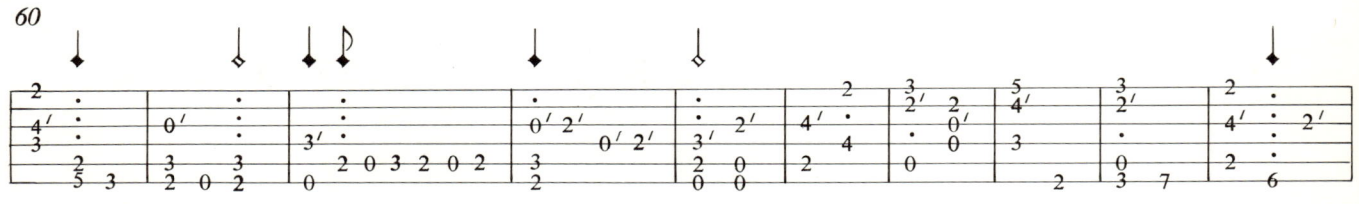
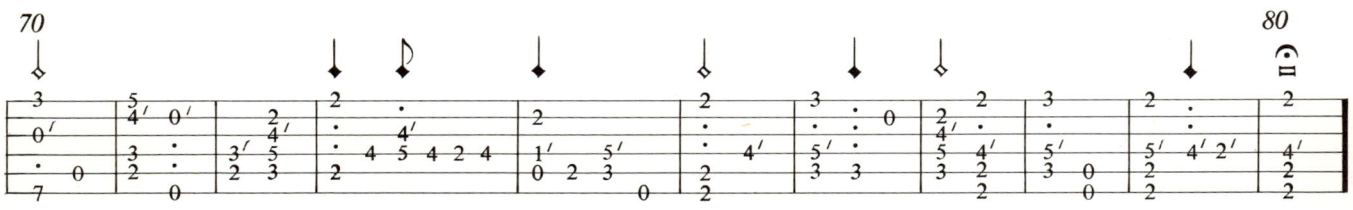

[17.] Fantasia por el sexto tono

Fantasia por el sexto tono, señalase la claue de Fefaut quarta en vacio.

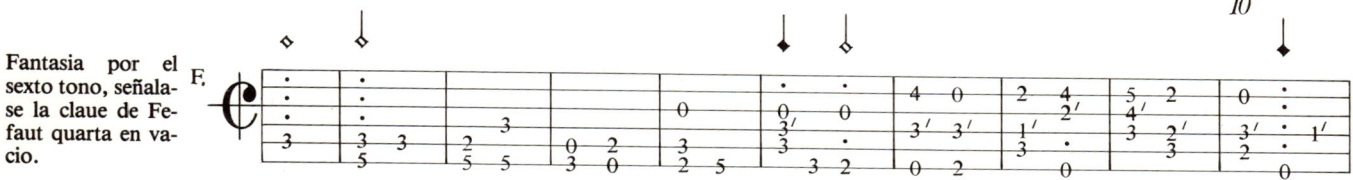
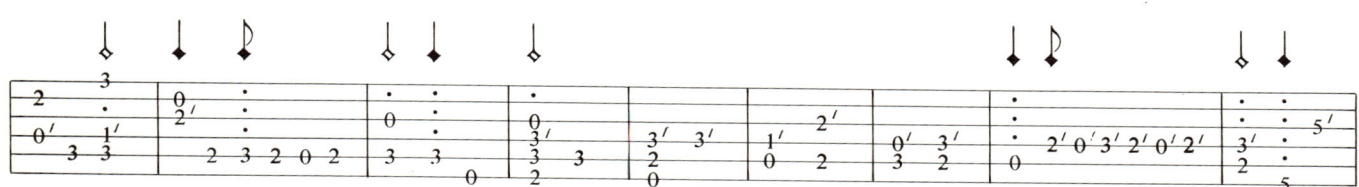
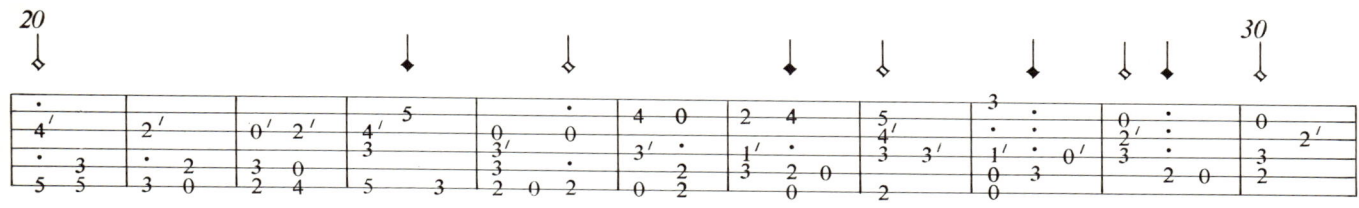
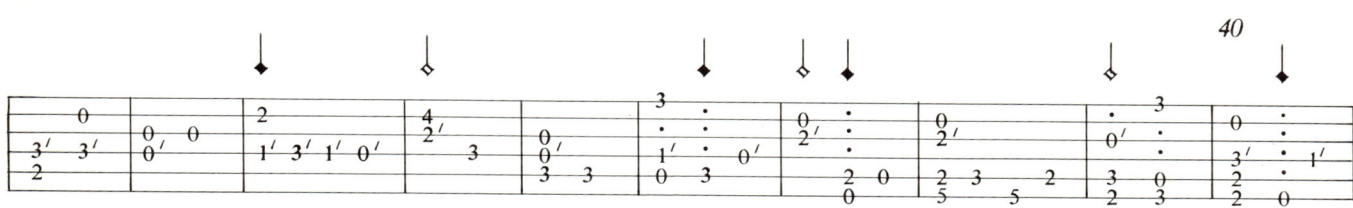
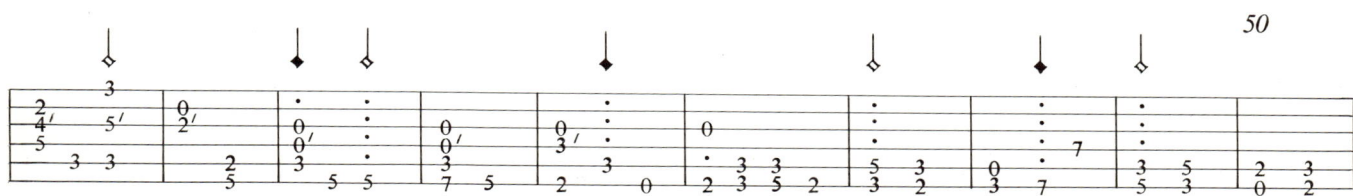

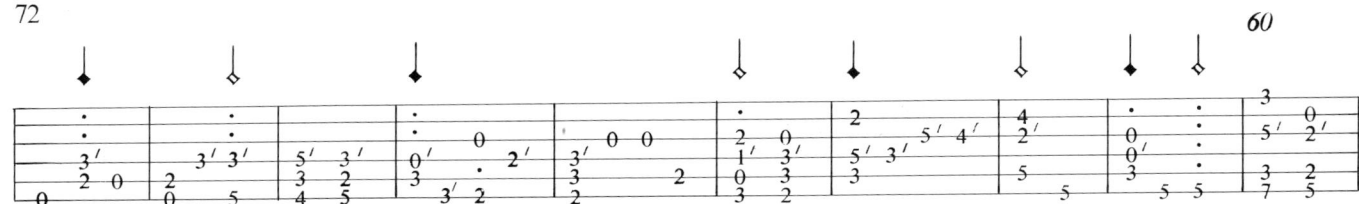

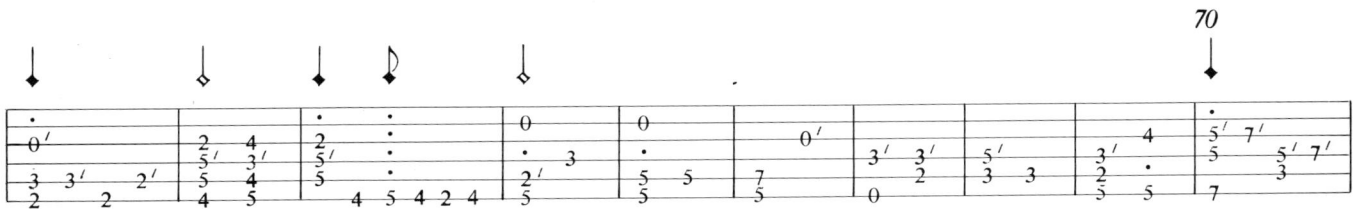

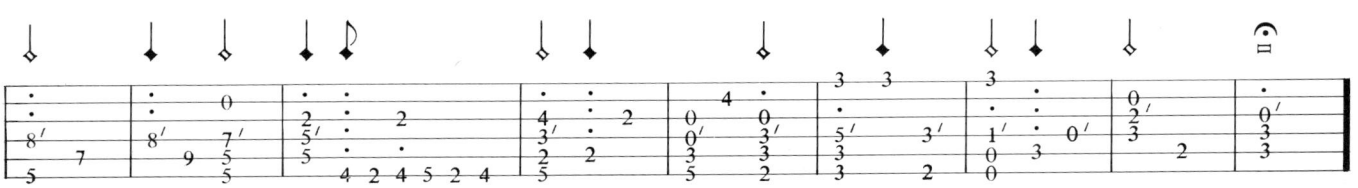

[18.] Fantasia por el primer tono

Fantasia por el primero tono a quatro señalase la claue de Fefaut tercera en primero traste.

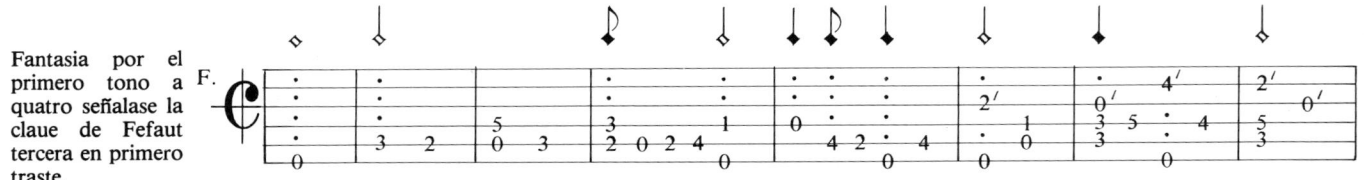

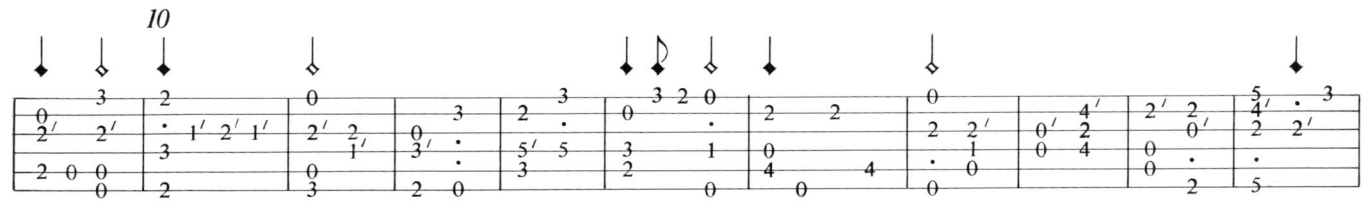

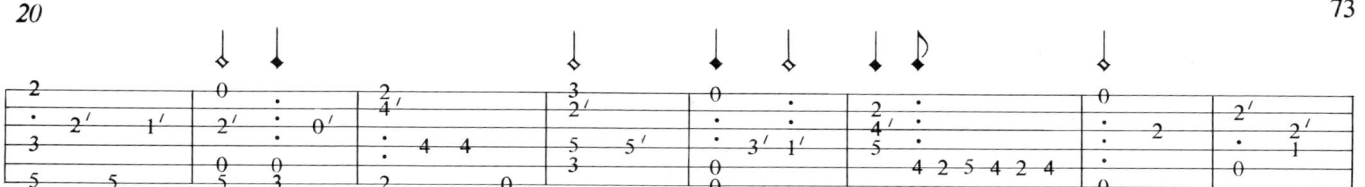
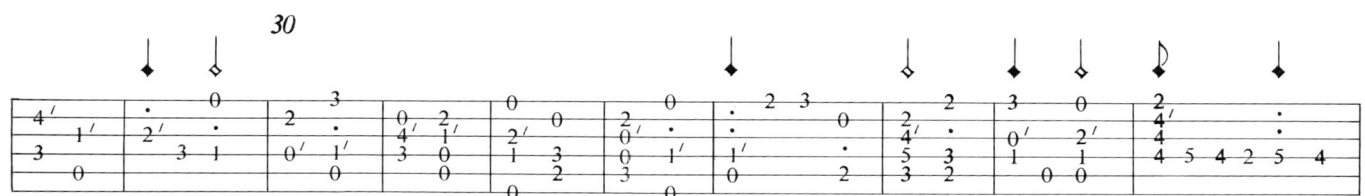
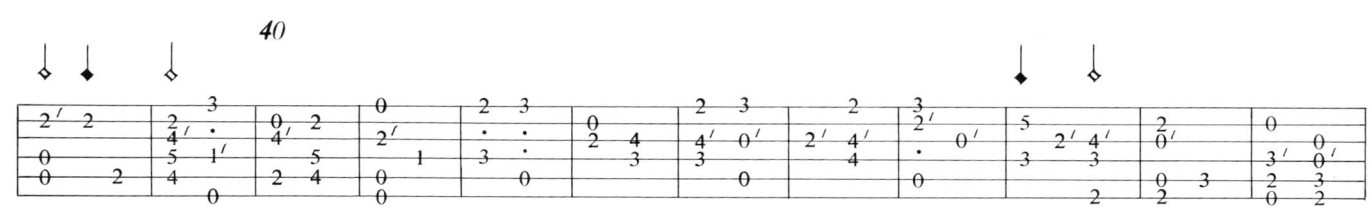
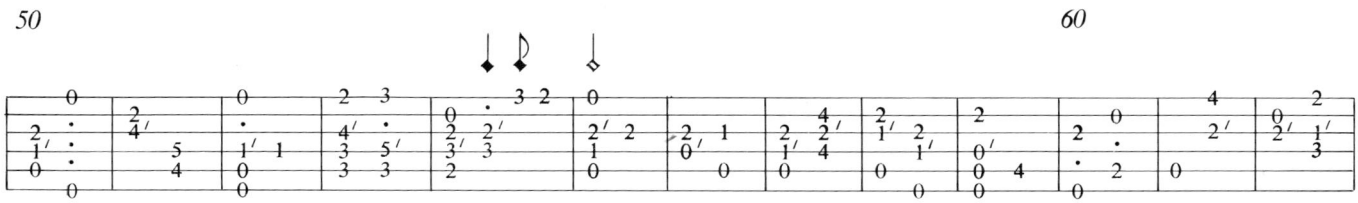
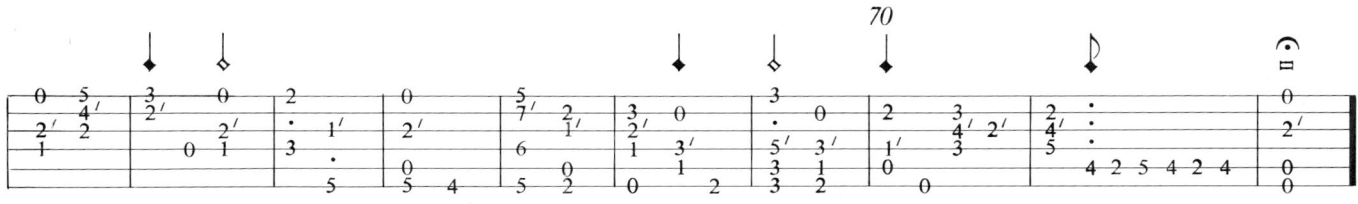

[19.] Fantasia [de passos largos] por el primer tono

Siguense vnas fantasias que lleuan ciertos passajes para desemvoluer las manas.

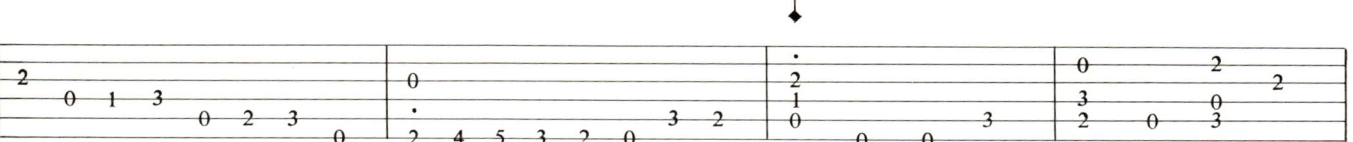
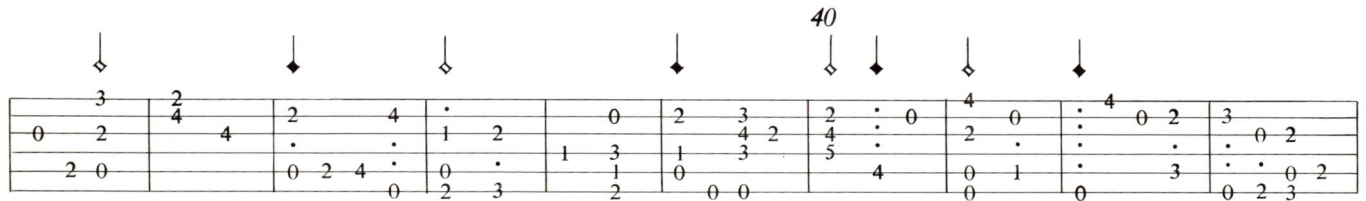
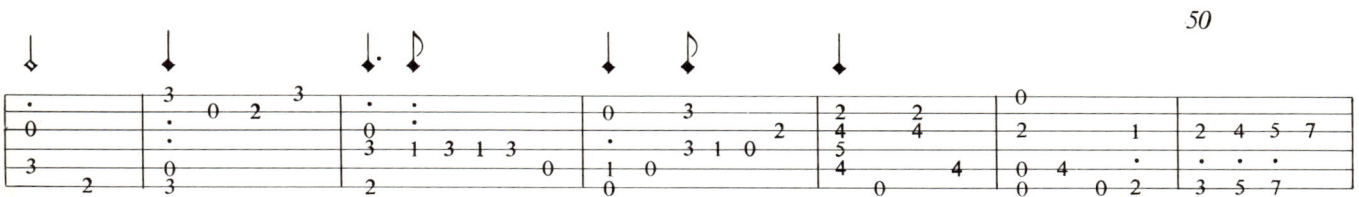
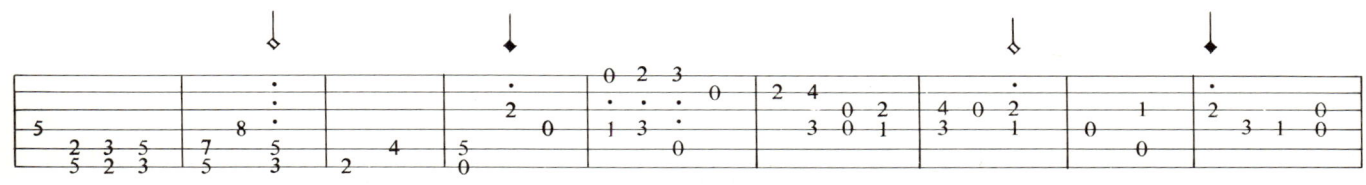
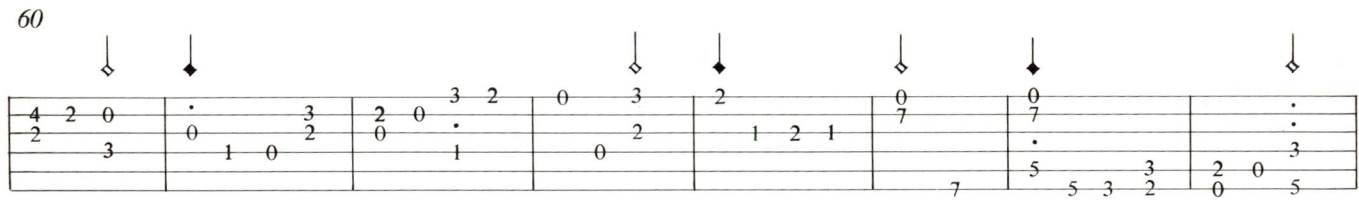
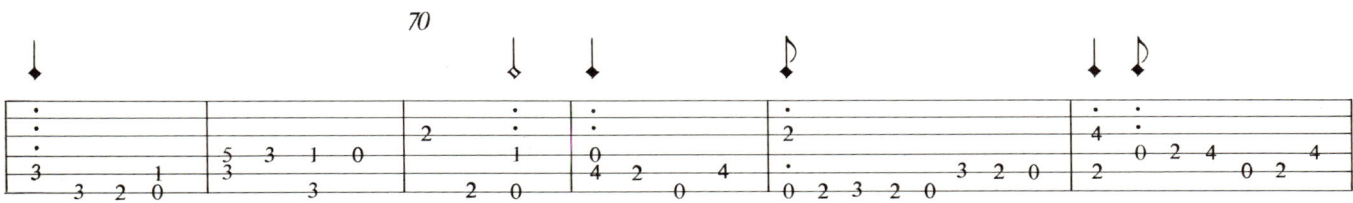

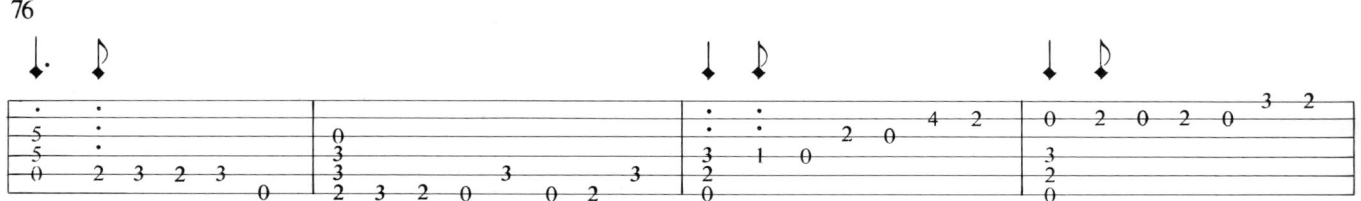

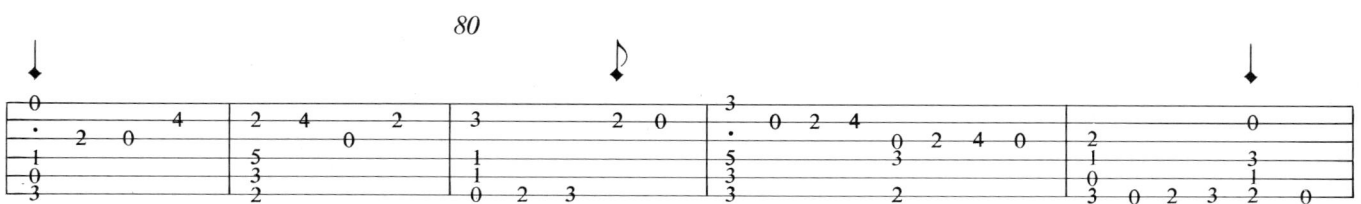

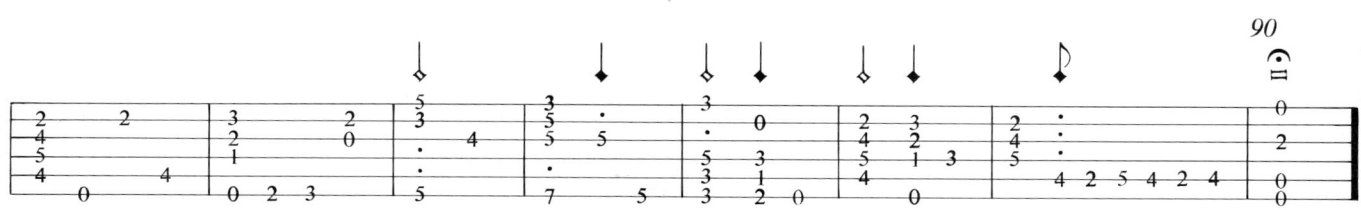

[20.] Fantasia [de passos largos] por el mismo [=primer] tono

Fantasia de passos largos para desemvoluer las manos.

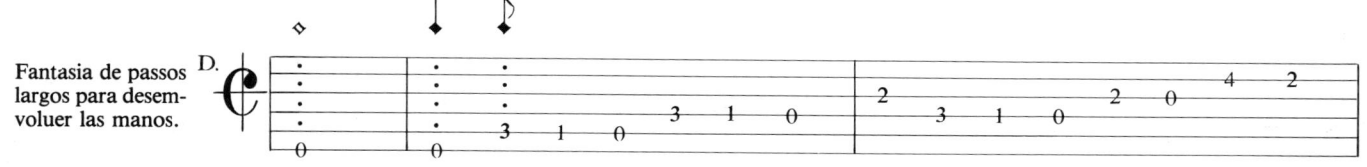

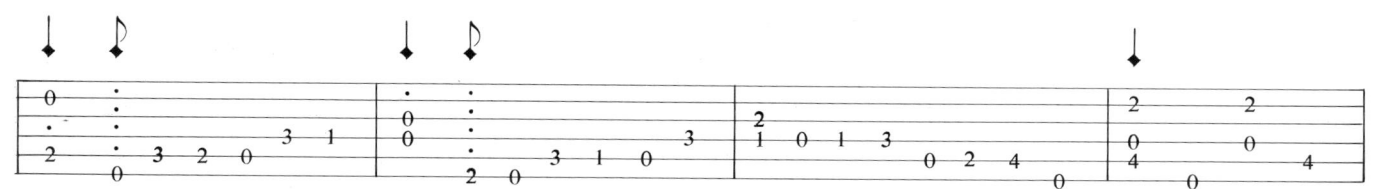

77

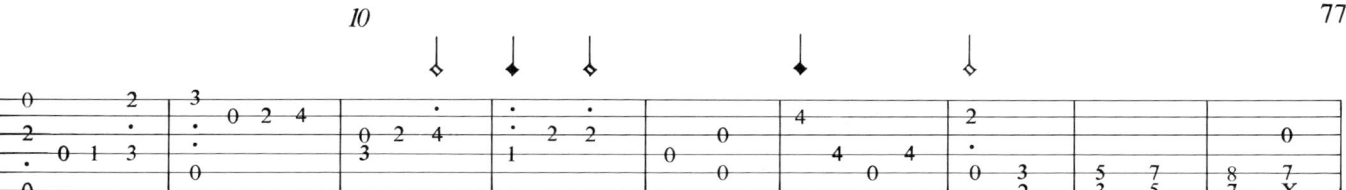
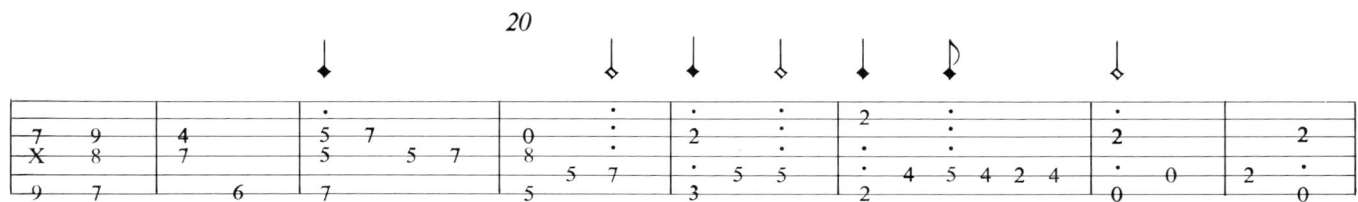
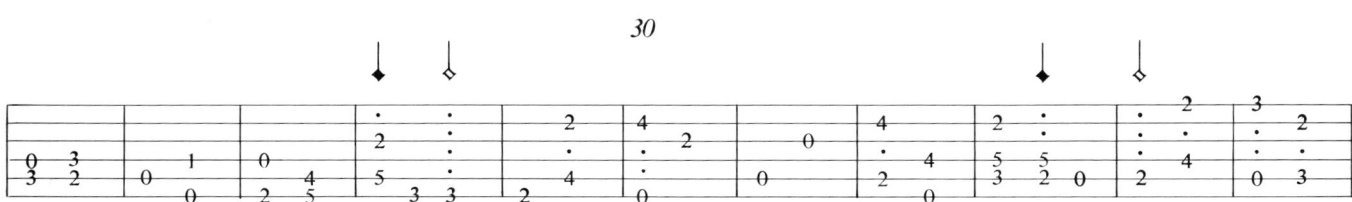
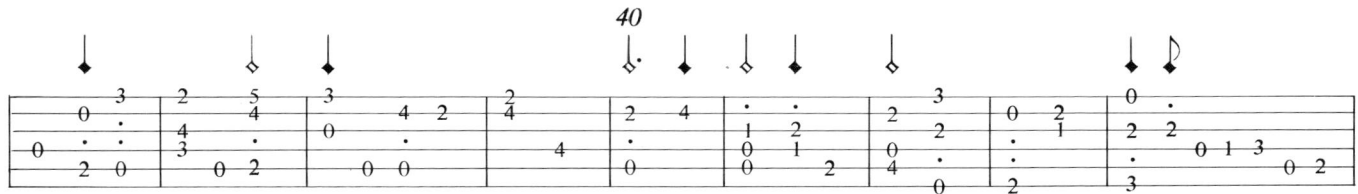
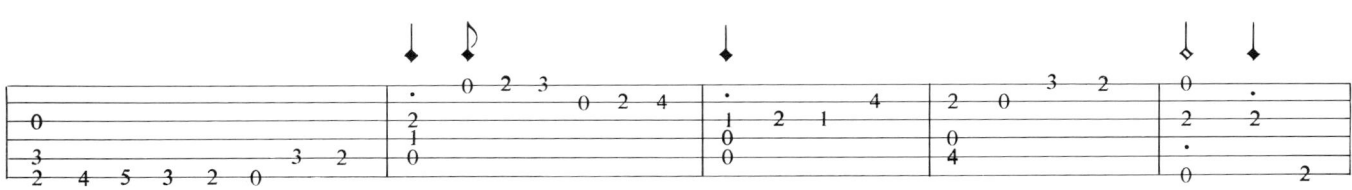

[21.] Fantasia [de passos largos] por el quinto tono

Fantasias de passos largos, para desemvoluer las manos.

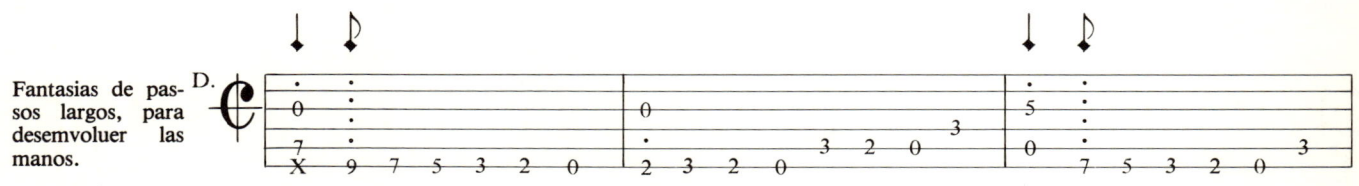
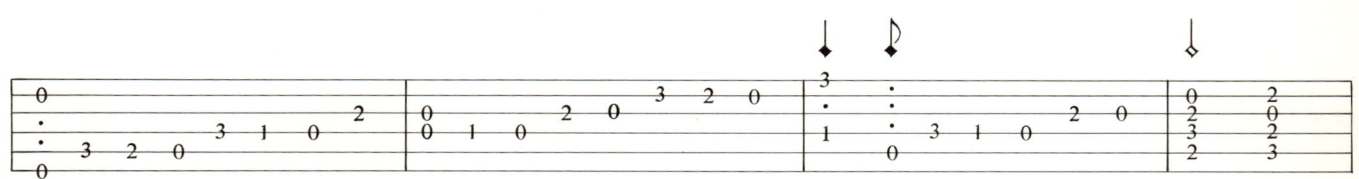
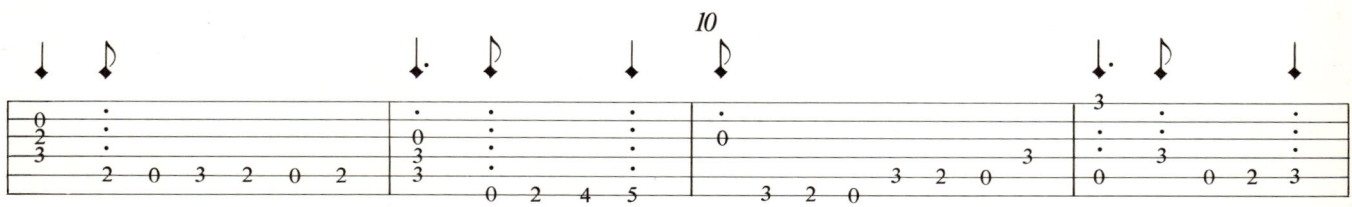
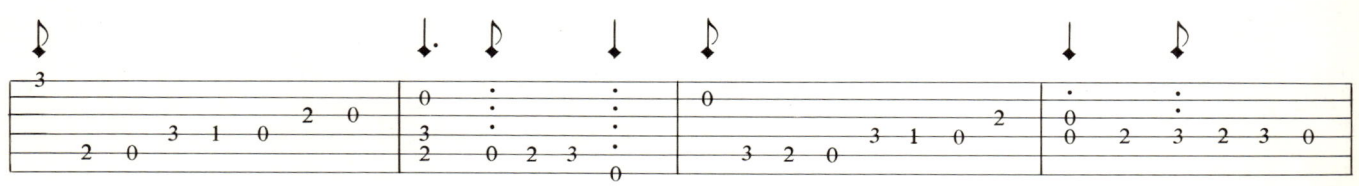
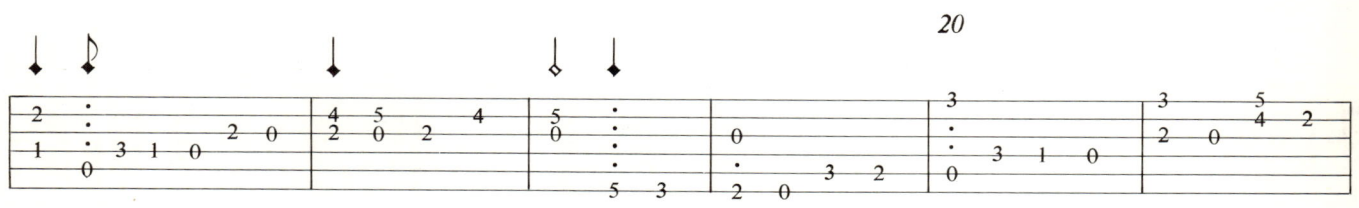
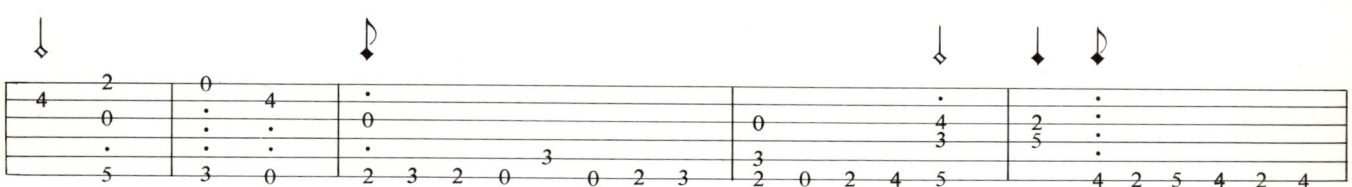

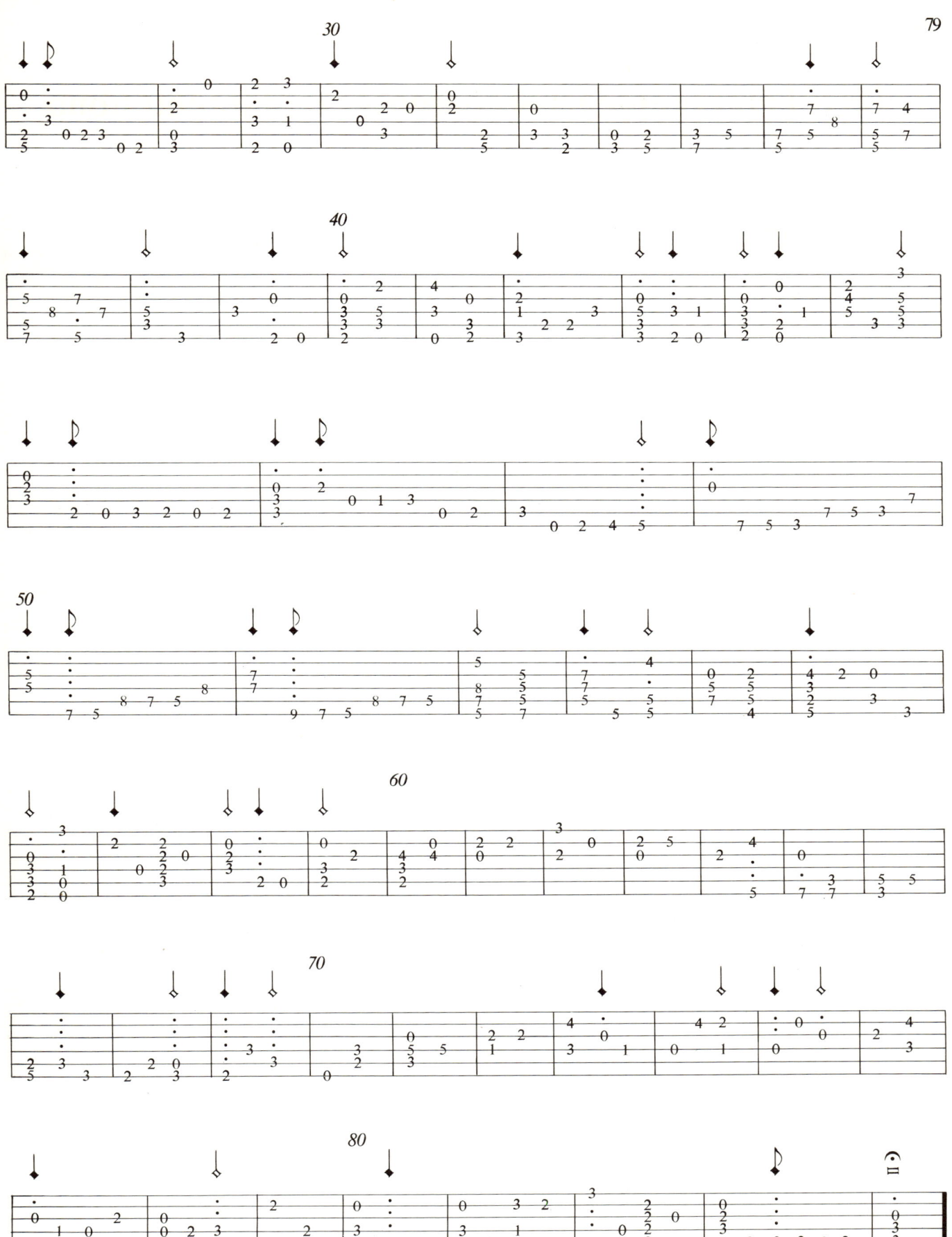

[22.] Fantasia [de passos largos] por el octauo tono

Fantasias des passos largos, para desemvoluer las manos.

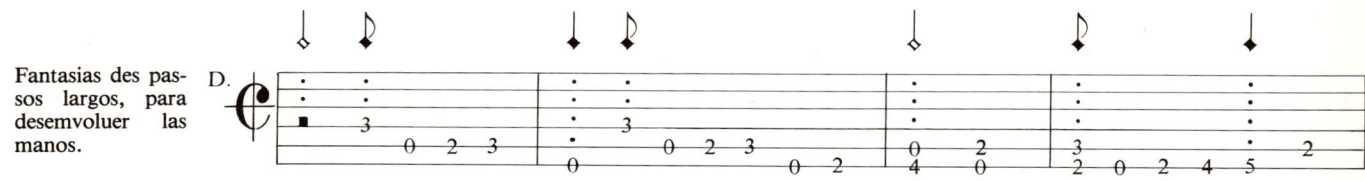
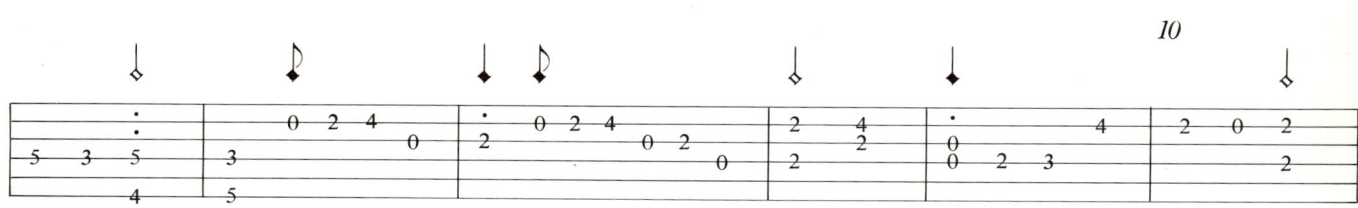
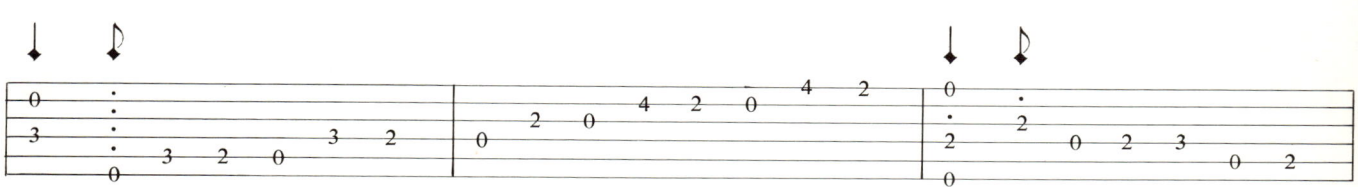
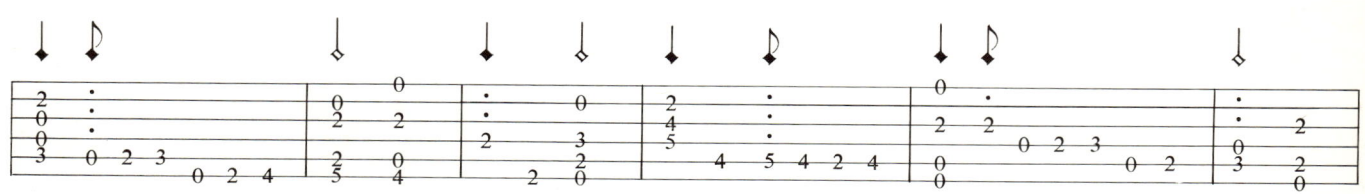
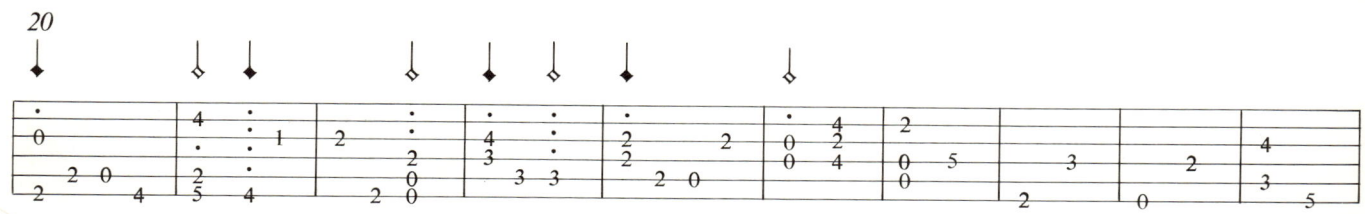

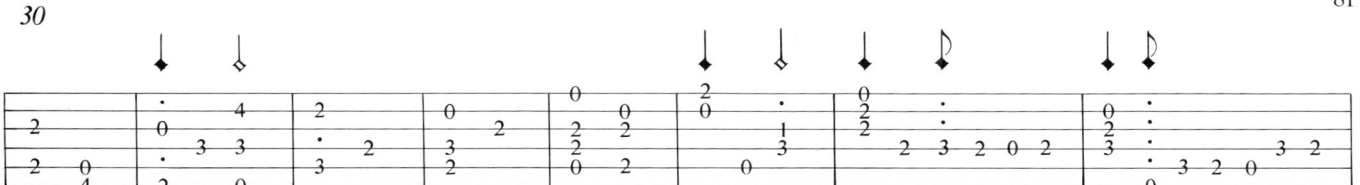
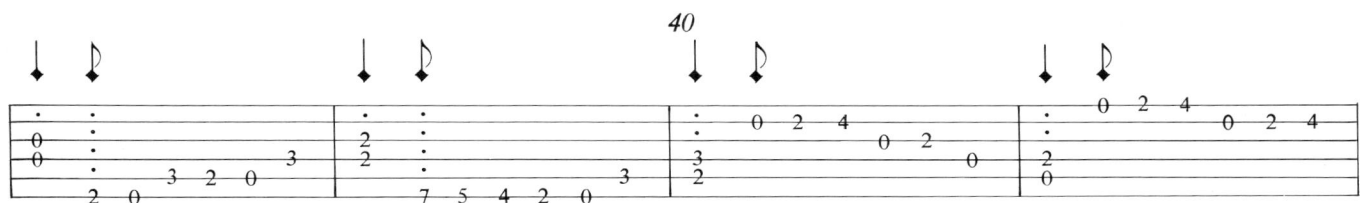
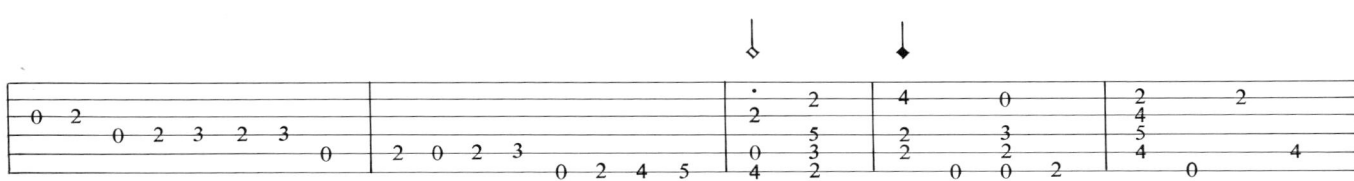
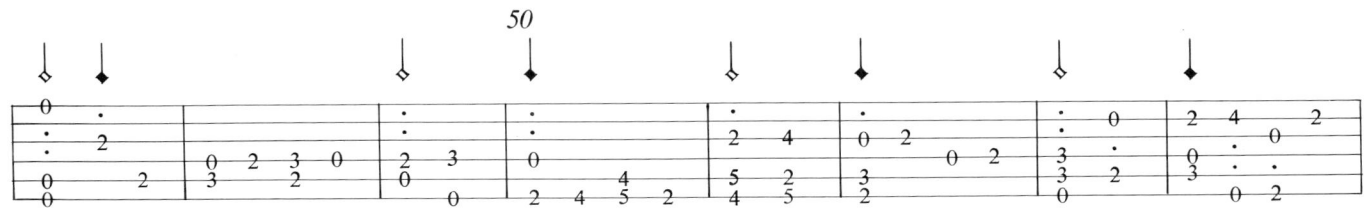
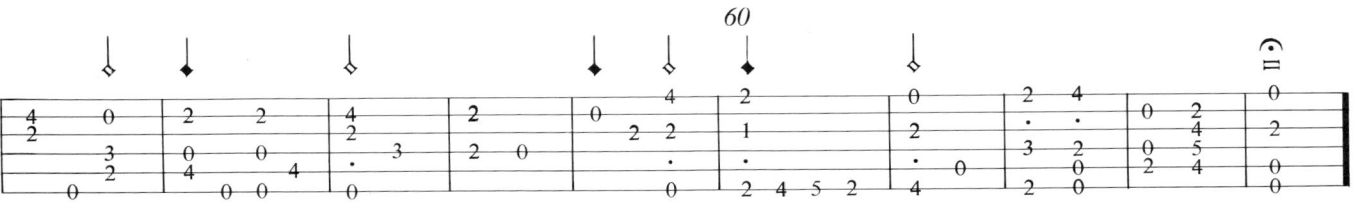